A TALE OF TWO KITTIES

Nick Harding

Mirror Books

This book first published in 2018 by Mirror Books

Mirror Books is part of Reach plc
One Canada Square,
London E14 5AP,
England

www.mirrorbooks.co.uk

ISBN 978-1-912624-09-6

"That cat is a bad one"

The Cat in the Hat Comes Back

Dr Seuss

PROLOGUE

This is a picture of me with my cat Barry. He is what's known as a Bengal. He's a pedigree cat, he has papers to prove it and a show name – Barry Kula – which no one uses because a) he was never registered as a showcat and b) it makes him sound like an obese American soul singer. Although Barry is categorised as a Bengal cat, he has never been to Bengal. In fact, when this photograph was taken, Barry had barely ventured 200 yards from his own home.

When he first went to the vet for his vaccinations, the receptionist looked and him and said: "I was expecting a more exotic name." But Barry suits him – he was going to be called Ian, but he's more of a Barry.

The photograph shows us at LondonCats, the biggest cat show in Britain. It was like Crufts for cats. In the cat-fancying world (which is bigger than you might imagine), it was a big deal and the highlight of the UK calendar. At cat shows there are no obedience tests or obstacle courses because you cannot easily train a cat to do tricks or be obedient. Cats are not subservient to their humans, no matter what their humans like to think. If a cat doesn't want to do something, it won't. You cannot bribe a cat like you can bribe a dog. The best you can do is trick it, but that only works a few times before it learns, and when it realises it has been tricked, somewhere down the line the human who tricked it will pay. Cats hold grudges and they plot.

Barry didn't want to go the show. It was my idea to take him. He was not happy when we got there and no amount of freeze-dried fish treats could lift his mood. Cats can be real party poopers. In the photograph, Barry was being judged for his looks, cleanliness and general demeanour. Although he's a handsome cat, he would be the first to admit that he has failings in the latter categories. I'm not being mean, I'm just being honest. You may look at him there and think "he looks clean, he looks fine", and by normal pet standards you'd be right. Barry is a nice, clean cat who doesn't smell. But that doesn't quite cut it in the cat-fancying world. At just over a year old – just before this snap was taken – he had never been bathed, but cats clean themselves and do not need to be bathed like their canine counterparts, which generally do smell, particularly when they are wet. That's why I wasn't too worried about bathing him before we went to the biggest cat show in the UK.

The night before this photograph was taken, however, Barry had been groomed for the first time. When I say "groomed", I mean half-heartedly brushed. Barry isn't one for grooming or brushing. He enjoys a stroke, a rub under the chin and a scratch on the upper base of the tail above the anal gland, but he's never been one for the full-on pamper experience.

By contrast, the other cats at LondonCats were into grooming in a big way. Many of them were preened to within an inch of their nine lives. They had special cat shampoos and conditioners, they had their nails clipped and generally looked and smelled very polished. Barry just smelled of cat: inoffensive, with a slight hint of fish.

The lady in the photograph is Aline Noel-Garel, a cat judge who flew to the show from Quebec in Canada. You can see from her blouse that she likes spotted cats, which is possibly why she awarded Barry a respectable fourth in his division in that particular round of judging (one of the eight he endured throughout the day). Another possible reason for the respectable mark was that Barry didn't attack her. If you look at Aline's body language carefully, she's leaning away from Barry, and her smile is a smile of relief because her judging round is over and she will not have to encounter Barry again. You see, LondonCats was Barry's first ever cat show and he didn't adapt well to the new and unusual environment. Up to that point in his short life, he'd only been in a car a few times to the vet or the cattery and had never experienced crowds. He'd met other moggies, of course. There are several in and around the area where we live, some of which Barry tolerates, some he interacts with and others he avoids. At LondonCats, Barry hated every other competitor. It was embarrassing. I was the parent with the socially awkward child at the party, the one who is only invited because the other parents feel sorry for him and who hasn't got the emotional intelligence or self-control to interact properly with the others. Barry was that child: aggressive, impulsive, petulant, unsociable and way out of his depth.

I'm not a cat judging expert, but I suspect his aggression may have been the reason the first judge he saw that day placed him last. And possibly because I'd failed to bathe him in cat shampoo, clip his considerable claws or make the kind of effort the other owners had made. Even in the household pet category that Barry was in, his fellow competitors had pulled out all the stops. One, a black beauty named Henry, was so sleek you could practically see your reflection in his coat. The pedigree cats were even more pristine. There were all manner of exotic breeds, from puffed-up Persians to huge

Maine Coons and hairless Sphinxes. There were even strange new breeds such as the otherworldly Lykoi, or Werewolf Cat, which looked like something from a felinophobe's bad dream. There were also cute but hard-as-nails Marguerites, the result of a domestic cat's union with an African Sand Cat, which is one of the toughest small wild cats on the planet.

For a cat like Barry, who had led a rather sheltered social life, it must have been like walking into the Mos Eisley Cantina in the Star Wars movies – full of aliens, strange smells and people wearing odd clothes (cat fanciers wear animal print and t-shirts with pictures of animals printed on them, often pictures of their own pets, fact).

You may also notice from the picture that Barry looks rather wide-eyed and tetchy. This is because, an hour before the photograph was taken, I accidentally doped him. I honestly didn't mean to. It really wasn't my fault, and it's not against the rules, which I discovered with relief later. It was the fault of a strange German man who arrived at our pen and quietly slipped me a small package to place in Barry's cage.

Alarm bells possibly should have started ringing, but up to that point Barry had been a bundle of anxious aggression and he needed something to calm his nerves. The package helped. Barry bent down, sniffed it, pawed it gently and promptly zoned out. His eyes got narrower, his breathing got deeper and after ten minutes he drifted off to sleep. It was the first time he had dropped off that day and normally Barry is a world champion sleeper. It's not unusual for him to sleep for 18 hours a day.

When the time came for his appointment with Aline, he was fast asleep and I had to rouse him. When I picked him up he was floppy and only the sight of a huge Maine Coon being carried past his cage made him wake up fully.

That was our first, and possibly last experience of a cat show. That I was there at all was a minor miracle. You see, the irony is that for most of my life, I hated cats and went out of my way to avoid them. I was allergic to them. They made my eyes blister. If, four years before, someone had told me that in four years' time I would be stood in a judging ring at the biggest cat show in the UK apologising for the behaviour of my own cat, I would have laughed in their face.

But that's the thing about cats. They work their way into your life, whether you want them to or not. They are geniuses of manipulation. Historically, it is what they've done through-out their own evolution. They are masters of exploitation. We humans think we are the ones in control and that we are the masters of our pets, but history proves us wrong. Cats have wangled their way into our lives and our warm homes and they have us right where they want us. Millions of us willingly spoon out the Whiskas without even realising we've been the victims in a vast inter-species deception. Cats take what they want and only give as much as they have to.

As American crime novelist and famous dog-lover Andrew Vachss wrote: "Cats are the lap-dancers of the animal world. Soon as you stop shelling out, they move on, find another lap. They're furry little sociopaths. Pretty and slick. In love with themselves." I couldn't have put it better myself.

So how did I, an avowed cat-hater, end up doping my cat – the second one I had owned – at a cat show? To understand that, we must start at the beginning.

CHAPTER ONE

FELINOPHOBE: ONE WHO FEARS CATS

Without realising it, cats have been lurking in my subconscious for most of my life. My first memory involves a cat. A lion, to be precise. In the memory, I am a toddler, I am with my family in Chessington Zoo, which was what Chessington World of Adventures was before it became a world of adventures. When I close my eyes I can see the scene clearly. My older brother, Alan, is in a pushchair. He is 18 months older than me, so I must be around two years old. Alan is wearing a bright red all-in-one romper suit and there are mittens attached to strings hanging from the sleeves. He is strapped in to the chair, which is on a grass verge close to a chain-link fence. On the other side of the fence there is a lion. It is a fully-grown adult male, replete with a huge mane. In my recollection, the lion paces up to the fence, turns, lifts its tail and urinates on my brother. The memory is vivid. In my imagination a strong stream of lion wee arches through the air and through the fence and hits my brother full on, drenching him. The urine is warm and steams in the cold air. The lion finishes, growls and pads away, leaving Alan sobbing.

The event and my memory of it are completely different. It did happen, but I would have been far too young to retain any clear detail about the fleeting event, and even in the less health and safety conscious seventies, I imagine lions were kept behind sturdy bars, rather than chain link fences. It was a story often recounted by my parents at dinner parties and as such, embedded itself in my memory along with a general wariness of felines.

Perhaps that was why, up until the age of 42, I had an innate aversion to cats and actively kept them at arm's length. Any contact I did have with them was undertaken with circumspection. For example, I once briefly house-shared with a couple who owned a Burmese kitten called Pavarotti. The rest of the tenants in the apartment adored it. I kept my distance and moved out soon after it moved in. Aversion to cats is not uncommon and mine stemmed from the physical reaction they triggered when I was in proximity to one. I was allergic to them, as are around ten percent of the population. Cats teem with allergens, which are found in their saliva, sweat, urine and in their dander, which is the name given to the cloud of dead hair and skin cells they leave in their wake whenever they plonk themselves down and start grooming, which they do a lot.

I did not even have to make physical contact with a cat to suffer the effects. If I entered a home where a cat lived and breathed in a few particles of dander, I started to wheeze, and my eyes and nose would run. For some inexplicable reason, in my early twenties, I developed asthma. The three things guaranteed to set it off were running in cold weather, short-haired dogs and cats. The cat allergy came with added discomfort because if I rubbed my face with a hand that had inadvertently touched a cat or a place where a cat had been, the skin in the corner of my eyes would become inflamed and blistered. It was an incredibly uncomfortable reaction which took hours to subside. On the rare occasions I encountered a cat and the cat scratched me, the results would be just as horrific. The wound would itch like an insect bite and rise into an angry welt. Consequently, I went out of my way to avoid cats. If I had to enter a house where cats were present, I would squirm uncomfortably, avoid touching any surfaces or my face and then change clothes and wash as soon as possible after the exposure.

Over the years my job as a journalist entailed countless interviews with people in their homes and on occasions I would find myself in a subject's house that was inhabited by cats. These were the worst jobs, and possibly the worst of all was one memorable assignment for the *News of The World* in 2001 when I was sent to interview a man called Kevin Carlyon who was The High Priest of British White Witches. Kev the Witch was a paranormal researcher and tarot reader from Sussex and had agreed to teach me some of the rituals and fundamentals of witchcraft and wizardry. He had an impressive burgundy robe and wore mystic medallions around his neck. I had arranged to see him because the first Harry Potter book had just been made into a film and the world had gone wizard crazy. I was working for the popular tabloid at the time (in the days before the paper's phone hacking shame and subsequent closure) and my editor thought it would be a good idea for someone to discover what wizarding was all about. Kevin raised an eyebrow when I turned up at his house dressed in a wizard's outfit I'd hired from a costume shop, which came complete with a comedy wizard's hat and a witch's broom. He also baulked at the huge stuffed owl I carried under my arm, which I'd borrowed from a theatrical props supplier.

"It's for the photos," I explained.

Kevin was very good-natured, and we spent half a day frolicking in his back garden, marking out pentangles on the ground, casting spells and generally pratting around. At one point, at the behest of the photographer who was recording my "lesson", we lit a smoke bomb under my robe while I stood astride my broomstick and pretended to fly.

"Call air traffic control for flight clearance," laughed Kevin, as I hopped around awkwardly while smoke billowed from under my cheap polyester outfit. I had wanted to be a journalist ever since I read the memoirs of famed war correspondent Edward Behr when I was 13. But my ambitions to travel the world covering conflicts and righting wrongs were never realised. The closest I got to a dangerous foreign assignment was a week in a holiday resort in The Gambia with singer Mark Owen from Take That. He was supporting a small animal welfare charity which looked after feral Gambian beach dogs and I arranged a trip to the small East African country with him and the charity. At the time – 2002 – Mark was pursuing a solo career. It would be another three years before Take That got back together.

I began my career in journalism on local newspapers in the 1990s and worked as a reporter, news editor and deputy editor on a range of papers in and around South London and Surrey before making the move on to national newspapers, where I worked on the *Sun*, the *News of the World*, and spent several years at the latter's magazine, where I found a niche as the print version of *Blue Peter*'s John Noakes, perpetually on the hunt for the strange and quirky. My assignments there led me to some strange places, including Britain's first nudist hotel (which was later exposed as a swinger's club) where I played nude ping-pong with the elderly owner. One week I'd be offering comfort to the man who left his wife after she went under the knife to have the biggest breasts in the country, the next I'd be flying down to Cornwall to interview a woman who spent over £1,000 on a pair of Ronan Keating's underpants. I was "an expert at the lunatic fringe", as one editor once described me.

I did showbiz interviews too. I dressed as a cowboy and went horse riding in the New Forest with Harry Hill, and I got bogged down in mud in a 4x4 with Ant and Dec. I also did serious stories and became a freelance writer in 2007 primarily to develop a more varied portfolio. I began writing features and news for more national UK newspapers including the *Independent*, the *Daily Telegraph*, the *Daily Mail*, the *Daily Mirror* and the *Times*. I did investigations and probing pieces into subjects including child trafficking, Islamist radicalisation, illegal blood sports and male suicide.

The reason I recount the white witch anecdote is because, like any self-respecting occultist, Kevin owned black cats. And not just a few. He had a houseful of the things, and while I was fine in the garden where their dander couldn't touch me, as soon as I entered his house at the end of the lesson I could feel my eyes starting to itch and my chest tighten. There must have been a fog of particles in there, clumped together in great clouds of cat dust. By the time I'd made my excuses and left, I was having trouble breathing and my eyes were beginning to close. It took a whole day for the symptoms to subside and several days for the spluttering and wheezing to fully stop.

***

Cats and I just didn't mix. But then cats have been the Marmite of the domestic pet world for thousands of years, at times either revered or hated. Their fortunes have swung between worship and persecution, depending on human attitudes towards them at the time. Leaving Kevin's house, full of snot and rash, I could almost understand why black cats have historically been some of the most victimised domestic animals in history.

The humble black moggy was almost persecuted to extinction in Europe in the Middle Ages by felinophobes precisely because of their association with witchcraft and paganism. And, given my experiences with the witch's pets, I suspect that those behind the cat genocide had allergies. The Medieval black cat backlash was fuelled by superstitious folk who believed the devil could transform himself into a black cat, and compared the way cats play with mice with the way Satan plays with the souls of sinners. Back then, cats and Roman Catholicism didn't mix, and the man who sounded the death knell for millions of kitties was the 13th-century Pope Gregory IX. He was the person behind the Papal Inquisition, a process set up to combat heresy. Before Gregory's intervention, responsibility for finding heretics lay with Bishops, but under the new system the Inquisition was brought in-house to a centrally run body staffed by full-time Inquisitors. As part of his mission to stamp out religious dissent, he published a decree in 1233 that linked cats – particularly black ones – with Satan and witchcraft. The link had been brought to his attention by one of his Inquisitors, who had investigated a suspected satanic cult in Germany and discovered that in the cult's rituals, black cats were used to represent the devil. As a consequence, millions of cats were tortured and killed, and hundreds of thousands of people who owned them as pets and pest controllers were accused of witchcraft. The satanic association stuck and, even in 1484, another Pope, Innocent VII, declared that the cat was "the devil's favourite animal and idol of all witches". The moggy's natural detachment and refusal to be trained like loyal dogs did not help their cause, nor did the fact that, while the Crusades were raging in the Eastern Mediterranean to recover the Holy Land from Muslim rule, Muslims tended to hold cats in high regard.

There is, however, a cautionary footnote to the tale of medieval cat genocide. A century after Pope Gregory IX sealed the fate of millions of European felines and dramatically reduced the cat population across the continent, the Black Death swept through Europe and killed around 200 million people. The bubonic plague was carried by fleas living on rats. The rat population had historically been kept in check by their most effective predator – cats. Without so many cats around, rat populations increased dramatically, which allowed the disease to spread as effectively as it did.

There are many recorded cat culls throughout modern history, more recently to control populations, protect wildlife and halt the spread of rabies, rather than to stop the influence of the devil. In 2015, for example, the Australian government announced plans to wipe out two million feral cats to protect native animals. The five-year extermination programme was launched after the government released figures which claimed that each feral cat killed up to 1,000 native animals a year, ranging from crickets and lizards to small mammals and even wallabies. Throughout history, when cat haters have needed an excuse for their repugnance, they have not needed to look far.

***

They say that in life you are either a cat person or a dog person, and as a boy, needless to say, I was Team Dog all the way. When I was very little we had a family mutt, Spot. We lived in a classic

1930s suburban semi in a place called Worcester Park on the borders of Greater London and Surrey. It was an idyllic place to grow up. It was affluent and quiet, and full of aspiring professionals who mainly worked in London. There were parks to play in and a High Street with a cinema. At home there was me, Alan, my parents and Spot, who was highly strung. He was only a small dog but was yappy and bad tempered, as lots of small dogs are. Spot belonged to my mother before she married my father and had Alan and me. After we were born, Spot didn't last long, on account of his disposition towards small children. By all accounts I tormented him mercilessly, tugging at him, chasing him and eating dog biscuits from his bowl, a habit that my parents tried to dissuade me from. It was this final indignity that made poor Spot snap. It was evening feeding time and Spot was minding his own business with his nose in his bowl, snaffling down his dinner, when I crawled over and barged him out of the way with my big toddler head (I must have been around two). All that pent-up rage and frustration was directed into a short, sharp bite. He caught me square on the nose and the blood started to flow. I screamed while Spot carried on eating, having dispatched the threat. My mum ran in, saw the bloodbath, gasped and collected me in her arms. I was rushed away and my (superficial) wounds were administered to while I sobbed hysterically and repeated "Spot bit me", in between dramatic chest-heaves.

I never saw Spot again. Like a South American dissident, he was disappeared. In a 1970s canine version of *Rendition*, Spot was secretly bundled away in the night, to an unknown location. He was never seen again. No one knew where he went, and for years it was never spoken about. Only later in life did my mum explain that Spot was taken to a rehoming centre.

I don't recall ever mourning Spot's departure and as the years went on Alan and I were allowed more manageable pets. We had a rabbit called Bonny, which grew as big as a cat. She lived in a hutch in the garden and had her own run. She was so big she was able to force her way out of her enclosure and was eventually dispatched one night by a fox following one of her regular escapes. I vividly remember looking out the window onto the garden on the morning of the incident and seeing two bundles of blood-stained newspaper on the lawn. Apparently, Bonny had been decapitated. I learnt an important lesson about death that morning: it is good for getting sympathy. As my mum explained to me that Bonny was dead (she didn't realise I'd seen the evidence from my window), she handed me a present to soften the blow. It was a book on garden birds and how to identify different breeds – not the most apt subject matter, given the scene of carnage in the garden below, but it was a present none the less.

Several months after Bonny's departure we got another rabbit and also two guinea pigs, Sooty and Sweep. Like most kids I was more in love with the idea of having pets than I was with the practicalities of owning one. I had to be cajoled into cleaning them out and, after the initial novelty wore off, I would only play with them periodically. My mum was left to deal with their day-to-day needs – a familiar pattern for a lot of parents.

What I really wanted was a dog, but not a snappy, violent little one like Spot. My dreams were partially answered when my paternal grandfather, Reg, purchased a greyhound. Her racing name was Melody Ivy (Melody denoted the breeder she came from and Ivy was the name of my late grandmother) and she was kennelled in Hersham in Surrey. She raced mainly at

Wimbledon Dog Stadium. Most Sundays, we would go as a family to the kennels and walk the dogs there. Melody Ivy was a successful racer and won many trophies. She was put out to breed by Reg when she retired. Dad, who worked as a printer in the newspaper trade in London on Fleet Street at the time, got his own greyhound. Her racing name was Munroe Melody – we called her Penny – and when she retired she came home with us. When my parents explained that we were going to have a dog I almost burst with excitement. I imagined how it would be: me and the dog, best buddies, sharing secrets and adventures.

I was around eight when Penny arrived and, much to my disappointment, the reality was a far cry from the dream. Like all retired greyhounds that have lived in kennels, she had adjustment issues and wasn't affectionate. She had spent most of her life living with other dogs, without the luxuries of a human environment and without constant human contact. She had never seen glass patio doors and often bumped into them in the early days; she had never seen or heard a bus or a lorry and was easily spooked. For a long time she had to be walked wearing a muzzle, as she viewed any small fluffy creatures, such as Yorkshire Terriers and Jack Russells, as quarry to be chased. She'd been trained specifically to chase after fast-moving small mammals. Often fellow dog-walkers would give us a wide berth and suspicious looks. Worse still for me, Penny didn't crave human attention. She didn't jump up and lick and she didn't climb on your lap. She was completely non-committal when it came to humans. Ironically, she was in many ways like a cat, which wasn't how I had imagined having a pet dog would be. But Penny was a loyal pet and lived with us for many years.

I had other pets throughout adulthood. My children, Millie and Lucas, had guinea pigs and eventually, aged 40 and divorced, I found myself living on my own, not too far from where I'd grown up, with my children staying part of the week. I thought it would be a good idea to invest in a tropical fish tank to keep the kids interested. It was about the level of pet responsibility I was willing to cope with at the time. I was one of the people who, in adulthood, lost the motivation and interest in keeping pets. For some people, something happens between childhood and middle age, and the magic and novelty of sharing life with a non-human wears off. Life takes over, cynicism sets in and pets take a back seat. Across the world there are millions of pets that find themselves in this situation. Once a valued and engaged part of the household, they are gradually set aside, usually as they grow older and start to smell. They sit in corners, sadly watching the lives of the people they belong to unfold around them but without them. They are discarded toys that no one can be bothered to play with any more. That was my opinion anyway, and I admit it was harsh and cynical. I know that many animal lovers share long and loving relationships with their pets throughout their lives and care deeply for their animals until the day they die. However, there are also tens of thousands of animals abandoned each year when owners no longer want them. In 2016, for example, in the festive season alone, the RSPCA rescued 25,000 abandoned, unwanted and abused dogs. That's just one species. In the same year according to reports, the charity reported that cat abandonment had reached "crisis point".

For me, even the fish, which came and went, were an inconvenience, and the weekly clean was a bind. I did get quite attached to a snail named Gary, though, who was eventually devoured by his tank mates. I assumed he was male because he would often climb up the tank and extend a long fleshy appendage out the surface of the water. Having no knowledge of gastropod anatomy, and ignorant of the fact that they are mostly hermaphrodites, I surmised that this was his penis and that he was waving it around looking for a mate. I later learned that Apple Snails, which Gary was, have a muscular flap called a siphon which they can form into a tube and poke above the water to help them get oxygen if they need it. Gary would often stay in his shell for several days at a time. Normally I would leave him to it but after one particularly lengthy period of inactivity I turned his shell over to take a peek. It was empty, save for his operculum (the hard "trap door" structure marine snails use to seal themselves in) and a rather overweight, happy-looking fish, which swam out. When I told the kids of Gary's demise, I gave them both books to soften the blow, thereby continuing family tradition. Gary's shell was too large to flush down the toilet so rather than the customary burial that the other fish had received, Gary's empty shell was laid to rest in the garden. I was sad to see him go. Some nights when the children were not there Gary had been the only company I had.

My attitude to pets was one of total detachment and it never entered my head to take on any more responsibility than I already had. I was unattached and free apart from my children, who I devoted most of my spare time to. I had a job that took me away regularly, sometimes at short notice. On one memorable assignment I travelled to a Buddhist monastery in France to interview the famed Zen Master and peace activist Thich Nhat Hanh for the *Independent* and the *Daily*

Mirror. Before I could speak to him I was required to spend time meditating, and stayed in a hut in the forest for several nights on my own, contemplating my existence and eating tofu. On a racier occasion I was dispatched to Madeira with the Peugeot rally team and got to ride around the course in one of their cars. Even if the fancy had taken me to get a puppy or a lizard, I was not able to look after anything more taxing than the fish. After Gary perished, I sold the tank and the rest of its inhabitants and the nearest I got to enjoying any animal company was when a fox nested under the old shed at the bottom of the garden and produced a litter. The cute pups would venture out and play in the morning and were a joy to watch, particularly as I didn't have to feed or look after them and could enjoy them in the knowledge that after a few months they would grow and leave their mother, and my garden. I was petless and fancy free. I could have got another snail, but what if it didn't have a personality like Gary?

***

Some people map out their lives with five-year plans and work diligently towards their goals. Others have a general idea of where they want to head and steer themselves in that general direction. I was in another category altogether, happy to bump along with the tide to wherever life took me, content in the belief that, to paraphrase John Lennon, life is what happens while you are making other plans. Things unfold as they should and it is often fate that leads us where we end up, rather than our own design. In 2011, when I was 42, I was sent on an assignment to meet the happiest people in Britain for a newspaper feature for the *Independent* and as I Googled away to find some relevant people to interview, fate was busy at work in the background. In my research I came across a Liverpool-based company called Laughology that was literally selling happiness to businesses and organisations. It had been set up by a former stand-up comedian named Stephanie Davies who had studied psychology and was an expert in the neuroscience of happiness and humour (incidentally, she did have a five-year plan). Laughology was a learning and development company. It devised training sessions and programmes for organisations. It worked in the corporate world with clients such as banking groups and telecoms companies but also worked in the public sector running such projects as community cohesion initiatives in deprived areas and courses in resilience and behaviour change for inmates in secure units. Underlying all the projects it undertook was the philosophy that humour could be used as a psychological tool to help people cope, change and improve their lives. As part of the feature I was writing, I spoke to Stephanie and she arranged for me to speak to one of the facilitators who worked for her.

As a freelance journalist, one of the secrets of success is to try and maximise the potential of the contacts you make, and when Stephanie explained about her business and what it did, I thought it could make an interesting story. I left the door open to meet up and learn more about her and Laughology, should I ever venture to the North West, which I rarely did. She also sounded like a lot of fun.

Two months later, however, fate intervened once again in the shape of a teenage gypsy bride named Sam Skye Lee. It was around the time I like to call "peak gypsy bride", when there was huge interest from newspapers, magazines and broadcasters in the excesses of traveller weddings, thanks to the success of the fly-on-the-wall television documentary series *My Big Fat Gypsy Wedding*. The focal point of the show was Liverpool-based wedding dress designer Thelma Madine, who created incredible outfits for traveller weddings, which were outrageously extravagant. The show's success lay in the access it got to the heart of the traveller community and the spotlight it shone on gypsy traditions, which had hitherto been completely alien to most of the British public, who were equally fearful of and hostile to travellers. Suddenly everyone in the media wanted a gypsy story, and when a colleague at a UK publishing house asked me if I could find a gypsy bride willing to tell her story, I got in contact with Sam, who was a normal girl (a "gorger" in traveller parlance) who had, at the age of 18, married a gypsy. She had featured in the series and Thelma had constructed her a monumental creation complete with LED lighting and robotic butterflies with flapping wings. The dress was wired with so many electric circuits and batteries that a fire extinguisher needed to be kept nearby in case it overheated and combusted. As is the case with most of the popular genre memoirs published, the book needed a ghost-writer. And that was where I came in. I brokered the deal between Sam, her husband Patrick and the publisher, and was signed up as the ghost for the project. It was my first book – since then I've written over a dozen.

Ghost writing, or co-writing as it is laughably called (in my experience there is very little actual writing from the subject) involves many hours of in-depth interview when it is done properly. A good interviewer will spend time drawing out detail and capturing the subject's personality. Consequently, the project saw me spending many days in a caravan in St Helens interviewing Sam. While I was there, to break the monotony, I contacted Stephanie again and arranged a late-afternoon meeting.

We met up for what was supposed to be a business meeting, but just before I arrived Stephanie had been offered her own book deal to write a self-help book based on the psychological model she had developed and so our appointment became a celebratory dinner. It was also an excuse to have a conversation that didn't involve weddings or gypsy customs. The first time I met her in person I felt a flutter inside. She was petite, stylish and very attractive. Her smile lit up the room and there was only the slightest hint of a Scouse accent. She was also hilarious company and fascinating. We shared the same sense of humour – slightly wrong and a bit dark – and were interested in the same things. The evening was lovely, and conversation flowed. At one point, talk turned to tattoos and I confessed that I had quite possibly the most effete tattoo in the world inked on my shoulder.

"It's a dolphin," I explained. "It was a surprise present on my 23rd birthday. A mate of mine took me to a dodgy tattoo parlour in Kingston and said: 'Surprise! Pick a design.' He said he wanted to give me something that would last. We'd had a few drinks beforehand and I hate letting people down so rather than voice my reservations, I feigned delight and went along with it." It was in the days before tattoos were ubiquitous. Only a few people I knew had them: these included "Uncle" Pip, a friend of my dad who sometimes babysat when I was a child and had a swallow tattooed on his hand, and my friend Steve, who took me to have the tattoo and who I worked with behind the bar in a nightclub. Steve had some sort of Celtic symbol on his arm and on occasion I commented on it. He took this to mean that I wanted something similar.

"Initially I thought about getting a Grim Reaper design with the words 'live fast, die young' written in gothic script underneath. But the thought of it mocking me from my 80-year-old withered bicep while I sat on a commode put me off," I shrugged. "So instead I chose something to represent the spirit of the age – it was the early 1990s, we'd just had the second summer of love – so I made possibly one of the stupidest decisions of my life and picked a dolphin."

I explained that dolphins were big in the early nineties thanks to a series of posters and photographic prints, mainly sold by a shop called Athena.

"When I was younger, I had one on my bedroom wall. It showed a pod of dolphins leaping through the bow-wave of a tanker," I said.

Dolphins represented spirituality, youthful exuberance, wisdom and freedom – everything I aimed for in life.

"I chose a design and a painful hour later there it was, etched in my skin forever, grinning back at me like a big, blue, camp imbecile," I lamented. The tattoo became a cross I bore as the years went on. I asked friends, "Tell me honestly, is it a bit girly?" "Yes," they answered. Later, when I started working in my first newsroom, I was christened Porpoise Boy. It sat there, its beak gurning back at me in the mirror as the free spirit it represented was crushed under the weight of career, mortgage and children. Athena went bust. Dolphins got a bit naff. My shoulder got hairy. I joined a boxing gym – a proper one full of men with shaved heads, broken noses and prison tattoos. On my first session there I wore a vest that revealed "Flipper". The owner took one look at it and smirked.

Stephanie listened to my story, laughed, took the piss and then trumped me with her own tattoo tale.

"When I was younger a friend and I went along to a tattooist in Liverpool and asked for something that wasn't permanent. He told us no problem, he could do us a 'five-year' tattoo that would vanish completely, so we took him up on the offer."

"A five-year tattoo!" I mocked. "There's no such thing."

"I know that now!" she laughed.

She picked a panther design, which is still there today, and which she likes as much as I like my dolphin.

"Why a panther?" I asked, expecting her to explain how it represented her wild side.

"I love cats. I've owned them all my life," she replied.

She talked about Fish Finger – her childhood cat, George, who had a weird thing for rubber gloves, and then explained that just a few weeks previously, she'd been out running and discovered the body of her most recent cat, Rocco, by the side of the road after it had been run over. My eyes started to glaze over.

"People think cats are boring but they are full of personality," she continued. "I could never imagine a life without a cat in it."

As she eulogised about the wonder of cats I caught the waiter's eye.

"Bill please," I said.

CHAPTER TWO
IN THE BEGINNING
THERE WAS ALVIN

Stephanie was too good an opportunity to miss, despite her love of cats. She had everything: brains, looks, ambition. I was smitten, and we clicked during that first meeting and arranged to meet again the next time she was in London. I was tasked with booking a venue and she explained her dietary requirements, which were ludicrously restrictive. She did not eat meat, was gluten intolerant, selectively dairy intolerant (as strangely chocolate and ice cream seemed to be fine), certain fish could spark a deadly anaphylactic shock and she didn't eat carbs after 5pm. On our first proper date I booked tables in three different restaurants dotted around the West End, just to make sure. We ended up in one overlooking the Thames on the South Bank. It was a perfect evening, full of laughs. I did my best to flirt but probably came across as clumsy and overly eager. Luckily, Stephanie's work brought her down to London regularly, so we met up again. We never discussed age, but I could tell she was younger than me. When it did eventually come up she told me she was 32 and I told her I was ten years older. Luckily, she wasn't bothered by the age gap, which I managed to bridge partly with immaturity. I put my cat misgivings aside and we saw more and more of each other and became a couple. It was a natural organic development and for 18 months we conducted a long-distance relationship between Liverpool and London which consisted of frequent late night drives up and down the M6.

I wasn't expecting to fall in love but Stephanie came into my life like a whirlwind and blew the cobwebs away. It's fair to say that before I met her I was meandering gently into middle age, with an expanding waistline, a badly conceived goatee and easily achievable life goals: mainly to be there for my kids, to earn a living and to get from one day to the next with the minimum of fuss and effort. But when Stephanie came along everything changed. She was ambitious and organised. She put her heart and soul into her business and believed passionately in helping people. Journalists, by contrast, are cynical and world-weary by nature. I began to see that life was for living and for having fun and taking risks. I worked harder, pushed myself further. I travelled more and developed more contacts around the country; previously most of my work had centred in and around London. I started some consultancy work of my own, advising people and organisations on media strategy, and made a conscious effort to say yes to every opportunity. So when she asked me to go to a salsa dance club with her, I readily agreed, despite having no experience or natural rhythm. I despised every second of it. At the start of the session there was a very brief explanation, delivered by an instructor with a fake impenetrable Latino accent, after which the dancing started. I did not have a clue. I was passed from partner to partner like a confused chimp with clubfeet. Each new partner greeted me with a look of pity and disappointment. Stephanie, meanwhile, sashayed from one snake-hipped lothario to the next. She had been trained in dance at the Liverpool Institute of Performing Arts (she only confessed this after I had a meltdown during the second hour). Despite the salsa, however, I genuinely felt that I had been given a new lease of life. Within six months I'd shed over two stone and was as slim and fit as I had been in my twenties. I changed mentally and physically. I became more positive and I trained harder in the gym. My physical transformation was helped by partially adopting Stephanie's diet. The first weekend she came to stay I did the quickest and easiest shop I'd ever done because I ignored 80 per cent of the aisles in the supermarket.

At no point during these halcyon early months of our relationship did any of the new experiences we shared involve cats. Whenever she saw a kitten on the television she would sigh and explain that she would get another cat at some point and that she missed Rocco. If she saw a cat in the street she'd talk to it and stroke it while I recoiled and refused to hold her hand afterwards.

Eventually Stephanie moved down to London and in 2013 we bought a house together in a Surrey village called Ashtead. To be fair to Stephanie, she had always maintained that if we bought a place together, a cat would follow. It was always a statement of intent, never a question.

"I'm allergic to them," I protested. "They give me asthma, they bring me out in hives… they make my eyes blister."

"You have kids, I'm allowed a cat," she countered.

"It's a bit different, and anyway, why would you want me to suffer? I hate cats."

"Of course you don't. No one hates cats. You'd just need to get used to it. You'll love a little kitten," she insisted.

The idea of me loving a little kitten was farcical. Some people melted when they saw videos of kittens. I gagged and scratched my arms nervously. I employed the use of lazy stereotypes to bolster my defence.

"Cat owners smell and women who own them end up sad and lonely. Besides, we live on a main road. It won't last a month," I persisted.

Naively, I assumed the frequent cat discussions were just banter. I was genuinely against having a cat in the house. Millie and Lucas tended to side with Stephanie.

"Stephanie wants a cat," they chided. "Why can't we get a cat?"

It was like Chinese water torture. Drip – drip – drip. Cat – cat – cat.

"We are NOT getting a cat!" I insisted impotently.

Alarmingly, Stephanie started looking at online pet sites and rehoming centres. I tried another tack. Stephanie's work took her away a lot.

"Who's going to look after it when you're not here?"

"You," she replied.

"No way. I won't have anything to do with it, and when you get back from a couple of days away it will have starved."

To this day I still don't know whether her persistence was a carefully contrived plan to wear me down or a Mr-Magoo-like stubbornness in the face of resistance. Whatever it was, my dissenting voice got weaker and weaker as I realised that Stephanie was going to get a kitten and there really wasn't very much I could do about it. When Stephanie wanted to do something, she did it, which in fairness was one of the reasons why I fell for her. I admired her determination but became a victim of it. I resigned myself to the fact that a cat was coming to live with us and decided that it would be better to be involved in the decision than not to be. I started to take my first reluctant steps into the cat-owning world and tried to find a breed that might be kinder to my allergies. Research was easy: I Googled the term "hypoallergenic cats" and discovered a breed called a Sphynx, which looked completely bald.

"Let's get one of these," I said to Stephanie showing her a photograph. "They're hypoallergenic."

When I started to look further, however, I realised that perhaps Sphynxes were not an ideal pet for a felinophobe. Although they tended to be less of a problem for people with cat allergies because they do not shed as much hair, they craved attention and hated being alone – and alone would be something our cat would frequently be.

I learnt more. Sphynxes appear bald because their hair is fine down. To touch they feel like peach skin. According to the Sphynx Cat Club, they are affectionate, sociable and intelligent. They are also vocal and enjoy the company of children. All of which sounded like hell to me. Their lack of a coat means there is nowhere for their sebaceous oils to go and so they need to be bathed. As I read on, I discovered some unpalatable truths about the genesis of the weird breed and the sometimes strange world of pedigree cat breeding. And it unsettled me. I'd never considered the ins and outs of selective breeding or how cats, dogs or any breed of domestic animal were created. I learned that the Sphynx's distinct look was the result of gene mutation which first appeared in a litter of cats in Ontario, Canada in 1966. A black and white domestic shorthair named Elizabeth gave birth to a hairless male, who was named Prune on account of his wrinkled skin. Prune was Sphynx zero: the first of his kind, the Adam of his breed. The problem was, there was no Eve and the only other female cat known to have the gene mutation that gave Prune his unique characteristics was Elizabeth, his mum. So, in a storyline that wouldn't be out of place on the *Jeremy Kyle Show*, when Prune was old enough he was mated back with his mother and their inbred offspring – Prune's brothers, sisters, sons and daughters and Elizabeth's sons, daughters and grandchildren – included some normal and some hairless kittens. These were then interbred some more over several generations to produce the Sphinx bloodline. While today's Sphynx breeders can chose from a varied selection, in the early history of the breed there wasn't so much a gene pool as a gene puddle.

Sphynxes were ruled out and Stephanie didn't have a preference for any particular breed. She wasn't interested in pedigree and said she'd know the one when she found it. In the end, she saw a kitten from a litter several miles away and informed me that it was a Bengal crossed with a domestic cat. I had no idea what that meant and wasn't bothered. For all I cared it could have been crossed with a Martian. The cat was advertised on Gumtree for £125. It was eight weeks old, had been weaned and vaccinated and was ready to go to its new home. Stephanie called and made the arrangements. She was given an address and arranged to pick the unnamed kitten up at the weekend, on a Sunday afternoon. She explained that there were two male kittens left from the litter and that we would have a choice. "Or we could have them both," she shrugged.

The day before we were due to get our kitten I was dragged around Pets At Home where the new arrival was bought a range of food, a bed, a scratch post, an array of toys, a litter tray, litter, a blanket, a brush, a carrier, treats and, to top it all off, Stephanie ordered it a cat Superman outfit online, "in case it wanted to play dress-up". All this was a new experience for me, though Pets At Home was not an alien environment. On occasion, I'd taken my children around the store because, with a range of rabbits, guinea pigs, chinchillas and tropical fish on display and no entry fee, it was cheaper than a trip to the zoo, but I'd never gone on a shopping spree there. I walked down the aisles, mouth agape. The automated toys particularly caught my attention. There was a range of different devices that ensured owners didn't have to interact with their pets. There were toys with rotating feather lures, ones with illuminated balls hidden in tunnels and even a cat version of whack-a-mole with a fake mouse that darted from hole to hole around a circular track. The FroliCat Dart Laser Cat Toy was an electronic rotating tower with a built-in laser pointer, for cat owners too lazy to wave a laser pointer around themselves. "What if the laser shines in the cat's eyes?" I thought.

Back at home, Stephanie unpacked the new arrival's paraphernalia and cleared a cupboard that would be solely used for cat-related products. I realised that I was largely a bit part in this pantomime and spectated from the sidelines, occasionally tutting and raising my eyebrows.

The following day – C-day as I called it – we were up early making the final preparations. Our house had a cat flap in the conservatory and I checked that it was all working.

"Why are you doing that?" asked Stephanie.

"So it can go out when it wants," I answered.

Stephanie tutted and said matter-of-factly: "It's a kitten, it can't go out until it's six months old."

"What?" I spluttered, doing the maths in my head. "It's eight weeks old. That means we're locked in with it for the next four months. And you'll be away a lot."

Stephanie nodded.

The thought of being confined in an enclosed space with a kitten for weeks on end filled me with dread.

"Who's going to look after it when you're not here?" I asked.

"You are," she repeated, followed by the refrain I'd heard repeatedly over the previous days every time I protested. "You'll love it."

On the drive to pick up our half-wanted pet, I asked what it was going to be called, but was told that the naming of the cat would only take place when the cat had been seen, as some names might not suit it.

After a short drive around the M25, with the carrier in the back of the car all made up with a cosy blanket and assorted toys inside, we turned into a council estate on the edge of Woking and found the house where the kitten was living. There was a sofa on the lawn and a gang of hooded youths eyed us from the corner of the road.

"Lock the doors," I whispered to Stephanie as we got out.

We walked down the front path and knocked at the door of a nondescript 1970s local authority semi. It was answered by a man wearing shorts and no top. A cigarette hung from his mouth and a perfectly round beer belly hung over his waistband. The thick smell of marijuana wafted out from behind him.

"We're here for the kitten," I said, blinking.

He ushered us inside and called up for the stairs to his daughter who, he informed us, was in charge of the cats. We were led into the kitchen where a teenage boy, around 15, was sitting at the table hunched over a joint. He looked up and nodded. An Alsatian padded in through the back door and sniffed my crotch. In addition to the dog, there was a tank with terrapins in and another with a large lizard. A long, languid, exotically marked cat slunk into the room too, and looked at me with piercing green eyes in that indifferently superior way cats do so well. It was a look that said: "I see you, but I don't care, I am far too cool to be bothered by you." Meanwhile its canine housemate continued to debase itself by attempting to poke its nose between my legs. The cat looked at it, and yawned, or perhaps it was a sneer.

I tried to push the dog's nose away and made polite conversation.

"I see you like pets," I said nervously. The boy blinked slowly with heavy eyelids.

A teenage girl walked into the room holding two tiny, mewing balls of fluff.

"That's the dad," she said, nodding towards the adult cat. "He's a pedigree Bengal, we have papers for him."

She placed the two kittens on the floor. One stepped back on shaky legs, the other bounded straight over to us. Immediately I was struck by the size of its ears. They were both as large as its face. It was a collection of triangles, with two large green eyes in the middle. It was in parts comical and striking. Stephanie melted immediately and let out an almost imperceptible sigh. I felt myself tense up. The bolder of the two kittens edged towards me. Stephanie bent down and stroked it. When she reached out to the other one it backed away.

The girl explained that they were the last of a litter of six and went to get the mother as well. The kittens' meows grew louder when she arrived and the shy one immediately sought her protection. I guessed that having lost four of her children already, she was naturally wary when strangers arrived. Her expression was saying: "Hang on a minute, I know how this goes."

The bold kitten's curiosity was undimmed by any memory of sibling snatching, however, and he was preoccupied with me. Despite my natural aversion, I couldn't help feel a few icy crystals in my heart melt. He was undeniably cute. But I couldn't bring myself to stroke him. Just the thought of contact made my eyes itch and I knew that the minute I rubbed them, the itching would start in earnest and within minutes blood vessels would start popping inside my eyeballs. The kitten sensed my reluctance and leapt clumsily at my leg, clinging to my jeans with his tiny claws. I shrieked and flinched. Stephanie laughed. "He likes you," she said.

I shook my leg and the kitten dropped off. The mother continued to watch, her calls to her kittens getting louder. I felt awful. We were taking a kitten away from its mother. I tried to justify it to myself and came to a realisation: I had a responsibility to whatever kitten we chose to make sure that its needs were met and that it was well cared for.

"What do you think?" Stephanie asked.

In a snap decision that would haunt me in the coming months, I pointed to the lively kitten and said: "If you're getting one, get that one." Then under my breath I whispered: "I think the other one's been drugged. Either that or it has learning difficulties."

The deed done, we paid our money and Stephanie picked up the kitten and gently placed it inside the carry cage we'd bought. It looked out between the bars, meowing loudly. At that point, every cat in the room realised what had just taken place. The mother started caterwauling, the remaining kitten shook and yowled, the dad hissed. I felt like a child snatcher. I felt awful. "What have we done," I thought to myself. I've no doubt that every caring pet owner who has ever purchased a kitten or a puppy from a breeder has had the same thoughts and emotions. What should be a joyous occasion is actually traumatic for every sentient being involved. The little kitten we had just purchased had, in the space of eight weeks, watched as its siblings had been taken away one by one – and here we were, doing the same. Taking it away from its mother and from the only environment it knew. Perhaps this is why we end up pampering and spoiling our pets so much, I pondered, because the foundation of most pet and human relationships begins with guilt.

I couldn't wait to get out of the house. I didn't want to prolong the situation for anyone and as we got in the car and drove off, I felt like a complete shit. The kitten meowed incessantly. Its tiny mews sounded pathetic.

"We've just torn it away from its mother, it's got separation anxiety," I worried.

Stephanie tried to soothe it but it continued to protest for the entire journey.

To her credit and thanks to her cat owning experience, she had made sure that the new arrival's needs were well met. When we arrived home a bowl of fresh food and water were placed in a corner and she put the carrier gently down on the dining room floor next to the bowls and opened the door, then stepped back to allow the kitten the space to venture into its new home on its own terms and in its own time.

"What shall we call it?" It suddenly occurred to me that the cat had no name.

We batted around a few options. Mine were mainly based on the number of laughs I thought I could derive from calling the cat's name out the back door months down the line when it could roam free: Kong, Kim Jong-Un, Kevin. Stephanie was largely in agreement that any name should have some comedic value.

"But not offensive," she warned.

As we were debating, a little nose poked out the door of the carrier and sniffed the air. Then, bold as brass, the kitten strutted out, looked at us and let out a purposefully, absurdly cute meow.

"Alvin," said Stephanie. "He looks like an Alvin." And she was right, he did. So that's what he became.

As it transpired, my guilt at taking him from his mother was misdirected. From that moment on, Alvin showed absolutely no signs of homesickness, yearning or grief. In fact he relished the opportunity to explore his new surroundings and trotted off around the house, sniffing everything, brushing against everything, marking out his new territory with a ballsy intent that said: "I'm here now, this is my manor."

I greeted Alvin's arrival with wary resignation. Stephanie had every right to a cat, after all, she had made the sacrifice and moved from her home in Liverpool to Surrey, leaving behind her life and friends there. The least I could do was agree to have a cat. I couldn't be resentful.

We lived in a Victorian house that had lots of nooks and crannies to explore, and within 10 minutes he'd managed to flatten himself and crawl under the door of the under-stair cupboard. Not wanting to disturb him, we left him to get on with it until, 30 minutes later, we had to remove all the junk in the cupboard to extract him from the furthest corner, where he was busy chewing on a straw picnic hamper. This became one of his favourite games and he spent many happy hours playing hide-and-seek in the cramped space.

Cats, by their nature, are curious and adaptable. While I didn't care for cats per se, I was and always had been concerned about animal welfare and I worried that Alvin would have trouble switching from a home where he was surrounded by other animals to one where he was the only quadruped. I needn't have worried. Alvin was stupidly confident.

After he'd spent a few hours exploring his new home we tried to settle him down. Up until that point I had deliberately avoided touching him. There was no denying he was cute, and when I looked at him, with his big inquisitive green eyes, some base instinct inside me was urging me to reach out and touch his fluffy coat. I fought the urge, fearful of the resulting reaction. When Alvin brushed against me, I made a mental note to put the clothes in the wash as soon as I took them off. We retired to the lounge, put the TV on and Alvin trotted in after us. He sat in front of Stephanie, who was on the sofa, and looked up hopefully.

"He's not getting on the sofa," I insisted. I knew that the dander and hair he was bound to leave would sit on the cushions like a booby-trap, ready to set off my allergies at some indeterminate point in the future.

Alvin attempted to jump up next to Stephanie, but the sofa was too high for him and he clung on to the side of it with his front claws while his back legs flailed around, trying to find purchase. After a few seconds he lost his grip and flopped awkwardly on the floor. I laughed. He looked at me indignantly, his large ears twitching.

"Don't be so cruel," said Stephanie, reaching down to pick him up.

"Not the sofa," I begged again. But I was outvoted. Alvin was placed next to his "mummy" while I kept my distance on the armchair, refusing to join in with the "family" huddle.

After a while Stephanie tutted.

"You can't just ignore him, you'll have to touch him at some point. He's a kitten, you won't be allergic to him anyway."

"I saw where he came from," I argued. "It was allergen central."

Stephanie got up, picked up Alvin, walked over to me and plonked him on my lap.

"Alvin, meet your daddy," she said.

I recoiled, then froze rigid. Alvin sat there and looked up at me. "Neither of us are enjoying this, let's just get it over for her sake shall we?" he seemed to saying.

Very carefully, and very slowly, I started to reach a hand out towards him. I don't want to be melodramatic, but for me this was a moment as climactic as the depiction of God touching the hand of Adam on the ceiling of the Sistine Chapel. I was reaching out to an alien species, one that until that point I hadn't been very keen on. I almost expected sparks to crackle from my fingertips. Alvin, for his part, sat impassively. First contact was made. My fingertips settled onto his soft warm coat and something spiritual flickered on inside me. I felt calm and warm inside, at peace. It was pleasant. He felt full of life: fur and flesh. I stroked and he accepted my contact. I felt myself relax. Just the thought of touching a cat had been troubling me, and before Alvin arrived I had been anxious. I had convinced myself that the moment I shared a space with a cat, I would balloon up in an explosion of anaphylaxis. But it didn't happen.

"Hello Alvin," I whispered softly.

I gave him a little scratch behind his ear and he pushed into me, intimating his pleasure at the gesture. He started to purr and I started to grin.

"You're not so bad are you little fellow," I said.

Stephanie was smiling.

"See, he likes you," she nodded.

"I'll have to wash my hands straight away," I said. I knew if I touched my face after touching him there would be trouble.

But the moment was undeniably magic. Alvin was loving the attention. Time slowed, and in that moment there was just me and him. His soft vibrations provided the soundtrack.

"He's so warm," I said absent-mindedly. And then frowned. He felt unusually warm on my lap. And the warmth was spreading across my thighs. Then came the realisation. I was snapped out of my trance.

"He's pissing on me!" I shrieked. I tried to back away, but he just sat there. I raised my arms in disgust.

"Get him off! Get him off!"

Stephanie was paralysed with laughter.

Alvin sat impassively, finishing his business, then, territory suitably marked, he stood, stretched, jumped down and walked over to Stephanie. As the warmth across my thighs cooled and became clammy and damp, I sat traumatised, wondering if I owned him or if he owned me.

CHAPTER THREE
THE GREEN-EYED MONSTER

As if the indignity of being urinated on wasn't enough, later that night, after I bleached my clothes and my body, I had another battle on my hands. Alvin had already decided that the expensive bed he'd been bought was not good enough. He had already conquered the sofa and, when it was bedtime, thought it was his entitlement to sleep on the bed. He struggled up the stairs, which was impressive given his size, and followed us into the bedroom. Stephanie put him on the bed. I took him off.

"Not the bed," I sighed.

The bed was a red line. I could almost suffer having a cat in the house, I could even suffer being urinated on, but the kitten was definitely not going to sleep in the bedroom. No way. Never.

"Poor Alvin," said Stephanie, as I plopped him outside the room, stuck two-fingers up at him and laughed silently in his face. I'm not a monster though – I placed his bed in the hallway with a cosy blanket and some soft toys, then shut the door.

The mewing started almost immediately. And it continued without letting up.

"It's his first night in a strange environment," reasoned Stephanie, "he'll be scared. Just let him in until he gets used to it here."

I was adamant. There was no way he was coming in. His meows persisted. Tiny scraping noises indicated that he was trying to get through the door. I put some earplugs in and eventually fell asleep.

Several hours later I became aware of something unusual happening under the covers. Something rough was rubbing against my buttocks. I was half-asleep and confused. Was I dreaming? I fidgeted and shifted position, rolling away from the strange sensation. A second later it started again, something warm, damp and fleshy was probing at my hairy bum cheeks. I woke and felt under the covers. I sat bolt upright. Stephanie woke, startled.

"What's wrong?"

"The cat's in here and it's licking my arse," I exclaimed, horrified.

Somehow – I suspect when Stephanie went to the loo in the night – Alvin had snuck in like a feline ninja and managed to clamber up the duvet and under the covers where he was busy grooming my posterior. I grabbed him and put him back outside.

The following morning, when I got up, Alvin was watching reproachfully from a gap between the hallway cupboard and the wall, where he had chosen to spend the rest of the night.

Later, as Stephanie and I had breakfast, I tried again to set down some ground rules.

"I really don't think he should be allowed in the bedroom. He can have any room he wants in the house. There are two other bedrooms he can go in if he wants to sleep on a bed, but he can't come in our room. I have allergies," I insisted.

"He's a cat. They tend to go where they like. Besides, he's tiny. He's just scared and anxious because this is all new to him," Stephanie said.

"I'm going to jam the door shut each night until he learns that he doesn't come in the bedroom," I concluded.

I did exactly that and the gap between the wardrobe and the wall in the upstairs hallway from where Alvin had watched me reproachfully that first morning became his bedroom. Each night I put his blanket in it and shut him out of our bedroom. And to reinforce the training that human beds belonged to humans and not cats, I forbade the children to let him into their rooms at night. This, I suspect, they largely ignored and deliberately left their doors ajar, hoping he'd sneak in.

The children first met Alvin when they came to stay a few days after he arrived, and immediately they were smitten with the kitten. At the time, Millie was 12 and Lucas was seven. We hadn't told them beforehand we were getting a kitten, because in the days before we got Alvin, I was still trying to talk Stephanie out of it and I didn't want to get their hopes up. The day they first met Alvin, they went to the pet shop and spent their pocket money on toys and treats for him. They played with him and Millie smuggled him into her room. They begged me to let them dress him up in his costume, but like a grumpy killjoy, I refused. This was honestly not because I didn't want them to play with him, but because I didn't feel it was dignified for an animal and I was pretty certain Alvin would not enjoy the experience. For the children, I suspect having a cat in the house made it more exciting when they came to stay, so that at least was a benefit.

Alvin continued to stake a claim to the master bedroom. It became a battle of wills. Each night I shut him out. Each night he would moan and mewl. Whenever he got the opportunity, he would sneak through the open door, only to be swiftly removed.

Stephanie accused me of being a bully when I ignored his

pleas. But I stuck to my guns. After a couple of weeks he grew strong enough to push the door open an inch and managed to slide through the gap. I put an old suitcase against it. A week later he grew strong enough to push past that so I wedged the linen basket against the door instead. When he could move that, I used the suitcase and the linen basket. It became a game of cat and mouse and a metaphor for the wider power struggle that was unfolding in the house between Alvin and me. He occupied every space. The armchair became his armchair. The spot on the sofa between Stephanie and me became Alvin's spot. My desk became his desk. The top of the filing cabinet became his. He was like a cancer, slowly encroaching into every space, suffocating me.

But begrudgingly I had to admire him. He was determined and confident and did as he pleased. I played with him and petted him but still maintained an OCD-like fixation with washing my hands after I'd handled him and not touching my face and eyes. On the rare occasions when I did, the itching started, but as the weeks went on, the reactions got less severe. Stephanie's theory about exposure seemed to work. The only times when I really reacted were when he scratched me, which, as he got bigger, he did more frequently as our play became rougher. Each scratch would swell into a bump and itch for up to an hour. I found that washing the wounds helped. To begin with, he was clumsy and harmless. He lay in wait under chairs and tables and launched himself at my legs when I passed. He did the same with the kids, particularly Lucas as he was the smallest human in the house. Alvin was finding his place in his pride. As the smallest member of the family he should have accepted his place at the bottom of the hierarchy, but he had ideas above his station. He targeted Lucas because Lucas was the next in size. He could see an opportunity to rise up the ranks. He attacked me too because he had eyes on a place at the top of the table. He wanted to be Alpha male.

When I mentioned my suspicions to Stephanie, she raised her eyebrows.

"I'm telling you, he is plotting," I explained.

"He's just playing. Do you really think he's trying to take over the house?" she answered. "You're being paranoid."

"Why doesn't he ever go for you then?"

"Because he loves his mummy!" she said.

I pointed out that as Stephanie had not given birth to Alvin, she wasn't his "mummy", she was his owner. But mummy or not, Alvin did dote on her, and he attacked his "daddy", which was fine and comical when he was a tiny, fluffy little kitten, but became more of a worry as he got bigger and stronger.

Still, I gradually adjusted to having a kitten around the house. Begrudgingly I allowed him into my home and into my life, but the bedroom remained mine. It was my citadel and I defended it fiercely. Eventually, when it became too inconvenient to barricade the door each night with bits of furniture, I bought a wedge, which I jammed under the door each night instead. For several weeks it did the trick, held the door shut and kept the intruder at bay. But Alvin's persistence continued. It is generally accepted that cats are inherently lazy creatures that tend to choose the path of least resistance. Pet folklore is full of stories of dogs that sit by their owners' graves, loyally mourning for years. One mutt in Argentina called Capitan kept a 10-year vigil by his owner's headstone and eventually died next to it, probably of a broken heart, or exposure. There are no similar stories about cats, mainly because at the first sign of inclement weather, a cat would be off to find another mug with a warm house and a larder full of cat food. Cats are not known for their willpower or loyalty, for that matter. There is a reason it's called dogged determination, not catted determination. But Alvin's resolve to get into the bedroom bucked the trend and was admirable. It also paid off. One night, after several months of trying, he finally beat down the last line of defence and managed to muster enough strength to nudge the door open and squeeze his lithe, thin body through. He was smart enough not to alert anyone to his presence and silently jumped onto the bed and curled up at the bottom, purring away softly like a well-tuned German car.

I found him there in the morning, looking sheepish, but grinning inside I imagine. He had that look in his big green eyes that animals get, which says: "yes, I know I'm not supposed to be here, but can you blame me?" I couldn't and I sighed. I realised that his will would not be broken. If I nailed the door shut, he'd find a way in, or learn to use a crow-bar. From that day on, the bedroom door stayed ajar and Alvin came and went as he pleased. The ironic thing was that he didn't sleep on the bed every night: some mornings we'd wake and discover him on an old blanket under the stairs, curled up like a feline Harry Potter. The cupboard under the stairs became one of his go-to places. It was where he went whenever he was left on his own in the house, which illustrated that despite his poise, he was still insecure. Whenever we arrived home he didn't bound out to meet us, he'd wait in the dark until he recognised a voice and then slip out from the gap under the door.

As he grew, his markings became more pronounced. The shadowed spots and rosettes that are indicative of the Bengal breed began to emerge on his flank. He was silver and black, with a brownish hue. He had a soft, spotted tummy and stripes on the top of his head that converged into one thicker stripe that ran down the length of his back. His legs and tail were ringed, giving the impression he was wearing Pippi Longstocking socks. When he ran with his tail up in the air he looked like a lemur. He still hadn't grown into his ears and his eyes were a deep, penetrating green that seemed both expressive and inexpressive at the same time. His fixed gaze rarely altered, but said many things. The "Alvin stare" could be unsettling or endearing, depending on the circumstances that precluded it. In one instance it could say: "I have seen something outside the window which is unfamiliar and I am now insecure and require contact and reassurance," or, in another, it could say: "I have just scratched you and drawn blood. This pleases me." To an outsider the difference was imperceptible, but I learned to read his very limited and subtle facial repertoire and I knew when he was being needy, when he was trying to be domineering and all the stages in between.

And then there were his meows. Cats communicate with other cats in several subtle ways, through scent markings, rubbing, head butting, body language and hissing. Meows, however, are only exchanged from kitten to parent in order to get food and then, when the kitten no longer needs its mother, meows are used exclusively as a way to communicate with humans. It's assumed the reason for this is because the cat relies on its human owner for food and soon realises that humans understand vocal communication better than scent markings.

According to studies, over several thousands of years of co-existence with humans and subsequent domestications, cats have evolved a universal language to convey basic commands to their owners, so when a cat meows it is ordering you to do something for it (when I discovered this fact, I felt uneasy. It suggests a level of inter-feline plotting which, at the very least, seems suspicious). The commonly held view is that certain meows convey certain meanings and I turned to the Whiskas website, which has a handy translation section, to help me understand Alvin. According to its linguistic analysis, a short, high-pitched meow was a standard greeting, a mid-pitched meow was a demand for food, a drawn out meow was a demand for something else, a low-pitched, throaty meow was a complaint and a high-pitched throaty meow was a sign of pain or anger.

I tried to use the simple guide but found it difficult to distinguish between the differences as each meow seemed to be small and hitch-pitched, and I doubted he was constantly greeting me.

My relationship with him was one of standoffish wariness and occasional grudging affection, while Stephanie's was based on adoration and love. I studied Alvin and monitored his behaviour, I tried to understand him in order to create a framework around which we could find common ground and make our lives together in the very least bearable. My natural journalistic curiosity kicked in. I was interested in him and his motivations. Stephanie, on the other hand, loved him unconditionally. I took the approach of a pragmatic peace negotiator, she took the approach of proper, dedicated pet owner.

"He loves his mummy," was the answer whenever Alvin ignored me and chose Stephanie. And it wound me up because, from my dispassionate, felinophobe, nonchalant pet-owner perspective, animals were not capable of love. They had instincts and they had social behaviours, but they didn't have the neurological complexity to have human emotions and feelings. This clash of views on the deeper emotional abilities of animals became a regular debate within the house, with me taking the position that Alvin could not feel anything other than basic instinctive urges and needs, which he displayed in simple nuanced communication (the Alvin stare), and Stephanie arguing that he was able to feel a much deeper range of emotions and connections including love.

The discussions went something like this:

Stephanie, watching Alvin climb on the sofa and sit contentedly between us purring: "How can you say that he doesn't love us? Look at him. He's so happy. He just wants to be near us."

Me, backing away from him slightly: "If he was in the wild, we would be his pride and he'd stay near the biggest cats because they would afford him most protection. It's a natural response, and nothing to do with love."

Stephanie: "But he's not in the wild. He's in a semi-detached house in Surrey."

Me: "It doesn't matter, it's his wild instincts."

Stephanie: "But he's not a wild animal. He's a domestic cat."

Me: "If you died and he was trapped in the room with you with nothing to eat, within a week he would start to eat your face. That is not the action of something that loves you."

Stephanie, frowning: "What are you talking about, you weirdo!"

It was a debate with a long history. Did we, as pet owners, anthropomorphise our pets and imbue them with characteristics they didn't possess in an effort to justify the emotional capital we invested in them, or were they capable of returning our emotional investment equally? I tended to think the former was true, and argued that Stephanie willed Alvin to love her because if he didn't, it meant that all the effort she put into him was unreciprocated and consequently, like the subservient partner in a coercive relationship, she was being taken for a bit of a ride... by a 5lb kitten.

This metaphysical bone of contention rumbled on and, my curiosity piqued, I started to investigate scientifically whether Alvin really did "love his mummy".

The pro-pet love lobby inevitably turn to dog stories to affirm their beliefs. Dog owners only have to read the story of Greyfriars Bobby to confirm their bias. Greyfriars Bobby was a police dog that belonged to Constable John Gray, who served in the Scottish police force in the mid-19th century and walked the beat in Edinburgh Old Town, a bustling part of the city where robbery and disorder were rife.

During the long cold nights, Bobby was Gray's constant companion. In documents, Skye terrier Bobby was described as follows: "Tenacious in character, distrustful of strangers but devoted to family and friends, he was courageous but not aggressive. No other sort of dog has more gritty tenacity, cockiness or sparkle than a Skye terrier with one particular noted quality – loyalty."

After his owner died of tuberculosis in 1858, Bobby's loyalty became a national sensation. Legend has it that the day after Gray's funeral, Bobby was discovered sitting on top of his master's freshly dug grave. He was ushered away but returned again and again and finally kept a mournful vigil on the grave for 14 years until he died in 1872. In Edinburgh he is a legend. There is a plaque marking the place where he ate, a bar named in his honour and a statue to commemorate him.

If true, the story seems to prove beyond doubt that Bobby loved his owner and that dogs can experience complex emotions. But did Bobby really love and mourn? Subsequent research suggests that the story of Greyfriars Bobby is just that – a shaggy dog's tale. In 2011 scientist and author Jan Bondeson published *Greyfriars Bobby: The Most Faithful Dog in the World* in which, as background, he found over 60 other documented accounts of graveyard or cemetery dogs across Europe in the 19th Century. These were strays, fed by visitors and curators to the point that the dogs made the graveyards their homes. People began to believe that they were waiting by the graves of their owners and so the dog was looked after. Bondeson argued that after stories appeared in newspapers about Greyfriars Bobby, visitor numbers to the graveyard increased, which supposedly created a commercial benefit for the local economy. Keeping the legend alive was good for business (a strategy that worked well in Loch Ness in subsequent years). Bondeson also speculated that in 1867, the original Bobby died and was replaced with a younger dog, which explains Bobby's supposed longevity.

But Bobby's story was just one. There are documented cases of elephants performing burial rituals, primates honouring their dead and pet parrots displaying jealousy... but were these animals emotional beings? Did they feel what we feel? These questions have puzzled philosophers and scientists for hundreds of years. They go to the heart of the debate about the ethical treatment of animals.

The bonds between humans and dogs are a product of around 15,000 years of co-evolution. The link between cats and humans is shorter. What effect has that had on our emotional relationships? Any devoted cat owner will attest that their pet fits in easily to the emotional framework of their family, but does the animal feel empathy with them?

Experiments have suggested animals can display behaviour we interpret as sympathy, generosity and even injustice. For example, in 2002, Frans de Waal, a professor of psychology at Emory University in Atlanta, studied how monkeys reacted to reward. In the experiment the animals were trained to hand a stone to a researcher in exchange for food. Initially they were all given cucumber. When a better reward in the form of a grape was given to some and not others, the monkeys with the cucumber became agitated and in some cases refused to perform the task. This reaction looked very much like indignation. In another similar experiment, carried out by researchers at Emory University in Atlanta, USA in 2008, generosity was observed between Capuchin monkeys trained to exchange tokens for food. In this study, the animals were offered two types of token. If they chose one type, they received a slice of apple but another monkey paired with them received nothing. If they chose the other type of token they also got the apple and so did their partner. Whatever the pairing, the animals chose the non-selfish option more frequently.

More recently, researchers at Goldsmiths College in London concluded that dogs have the ability to express empathy, which is a sophisticated "secondary emotion". In the study they discovered that dogs oriented toward their owner or a stranger more often when the person was pretending to cry than when they were talking or humming. Moreover, when the stranger pretended to cry, rather than approaching their owner for comfort, dogs sniffed, nuzzled and licked the stranger instead. The study concluded that the behaviour was consistent with an expression of empathic concern, but also pointed out that it could be interpreted as "emotional contagion coupled with a previous learning history in which they have been rewarded for approaching distressed human companions".

Was the same true for Alvin? Could he empathise with my situation? I thought not. If he could, he would have understood my aversion to having him in the bedroom.

I spoke to Dr Paul Morris, principal psychology lecturer at the University of Portsmouth in the UK and one of the world's leading researchers into emotions in non-primates. His work focused on secondary emotions in animals. Mammals all display instinctive emotions vital for survival such as fear and aggression, but the more complex emotions – secondary emotions such as love and jealousy – are used for social purposes. Neurologically, all mammals, whether human or mouse, share the anatomical structures in the brain where secondary emotions reside.

Dr Morris explained that without the ability to experience secondary emotions, animals that live in groups and rely on group structures for survival would not be able to co-habit.

"The neural equipment is there for doing some sophisticated stuff," he told me. "Primary emotions like anger and fear keep the animal safe but secondary emotions like jealousy, guilt and empathy are social emotions for regulating social interactions. Animals live in sophisticated groups. How is their behaviour being regulated within those groups? If it isn't being done by emotions what is it being done by?

"For communities of animals to cohere they need to have strong social bonds and a mutual interest. They need love: love between each other and love in the form of bonds to their offspring. It would be weird if animals that live in packs didn't have love and affection for each other.

"From a scientific perspective there has always been a reluctance to prove that animals do sophisticated things and a worry about anthropomorphising them. I started off with the facts that animals do sophisticated things: they perform co-operative hunting, they co-raise offspring, they live in hierarchical structures. If it is not emotions regulating these behaviours, are they sitting down and discussing them? I think emotions are a more parsimonious explanation to how they are achieving this level of sophistication. The incontrovertible fact is that they are doing sophisticated stuff in terms of social structure and interaction."

Dr Morris seemed to be suggesting that perhaps I underestimated Alvin's emotional range, a thought that undermined my fundamental assumptions about him, his needs and his place in our family.

The one element I held on to was that small cats, of the type domestic cats are evolved from, are inherently solitary creatures and so do not need the social mechanisms required by other mammals that live in large groups. Only some feral cats live in communities, most household cats prefer to be alone. There is usually a very good evolutionary reason for each specific emotion. In the case of empathy, it is important for an animal to be able to identify another animal in distress. And jealousy is important for protecting a mate and also for protecting other social relationships within a group. But love? Cats don't bond for life, and most do not live in close-knit communities.

Dr Morris explained further: "Animals form alliances within groups, some people may interpret these as friendships. To be aware of those alliances and to be protective of them is very sensible. If you are attacked by someone higher up in the hierarchy or if someone challenges your position from lower down, it is important to have solidarity with others who are going to support you or at least not join in with the attack."

He concluded that although animal and human emotions may feel different, he believed they are deeply related.

"I would never claim that dog jealousy is like human jealousy," he said. "I think in animals, emotion is in the moment, but there is something prototypical about it." Meaning, I assumed, that there was some kind of shared emotional ancestry between species.

My preoccupation with whether Alvin really did "love his mummy" troubled me for months and eventually I was given the opportunity to put the question to one of the most iconic naturalists and broadcasters in the world. I was offered the chance of an interview with Sir David Attenborough and as part of a wide-ranging set of topics that included climate change, population control and species conservation, I thought I'd also use the opportunity to find out his views on whether animals could display emotions, and so finally put a family dispute to bed. Who could argue with Sir David, after all?

From a journalistic point of view, the practice of using interview time with national icons to solve personal dilemmas is usually frowned upon, but I was not the first journalist to slot a personal question into an interview and I figured that the subject I was quizzing Sir David about was interesting and relevant enough to millions of animal lovers to be a valid discussion point. I wasn't asking about Alvin specifically, more for a general view.

I met Sir David in a private room in Kew Gardens in London where he is a patron. He was doing the interview to promote a series he had filmed about plants and, after a brief introduction and screening, I sat down with him in a quiet corner and explained what an honour it was to meet him. Over the years I had met and interviewed hundreds of public figures, including politicians, business leaders and celebrities. Sir David was as near to a legend as you could get and there was something special about being in his presence. Like millions of others I had grown up watching his natural history documentaries. When he spoke to say hello, his voice was so recognisable and familiar it made the hairs on my arms stand up.

Despite the physical challenges he was facing (in his late eighties, he looked frail and had trouble walking), Sir David's mind was as sharp, analytical and engaged as ever. His breadth of knowledge and experience was incredible. When we discussed climate change and the future, he spoke with urgency and concern.

"I am not optimistic," he told me.

We discussed a recent trip he'd taken to the Galapagos Islands where he was reunited with Lonesome George, the last known Pinta giant tortoise, which he had filmed in a previous series. Soon after the reunion, Lonesome George died.

"It was almost the last shot we got. I crawled up alongside him and he looked at me. He was very old and creaky, just like me. I said a few words to him, he didn't reply. He was, in a scientific sense, already dead, because a lonely male without a female has no future."

Sir David, who lost his wife in 1997 and lived alone, spoke the words softly. Could the sentimentality that humans feel for animals like Lonesome George be reciprocated? It seemed like the perfect time to ask my question. Could they love us?

"It is possible to over-anthropomorphise animals," Sir David explained. "You have to define what you mean by love. Of course there are bonds between a dog and its master but I don't think animals are capable of love."

I allowed myself a brief smirk. He had given me the answer I'd been looking for. Evidently Alvin didn't love his mummy after all, and I delighted in explaining this to Stephanie later that evening over dinner.

"You can't argue with Sir David," I said triumphantly to her that night.

"Alvin loves us," she countered. Apparently you can argue with Sir David.

All the while Alvin was by her feet, constantly brushing his flanks against her, purring and eyeing me reproachfully.

***

As it transpired, my victory was empty and over the following weeks it became evident that the argument over whether Alvin could experience love or not was moot, because he started to display another secondary emotion instead. Alvin became insanely jealous.

It started at night and confirmed my deeply held concerns about him being allowed in the bedroom. He took to sleeping on the bed every night, positioning himself in the middle between Stephanie and me. At a time when we should have been enjoying the romantic possibilities of our first home together, my advances were more often than not frustrated by a bad-tempered creature that attacked me if I dared move towards Stephanie. After fending me off, he curled up next to her and purred. Often, if I really pushed him and put an arm around Stephanie, he went into a frenzy and leapt at my head before running around the room, stopping in front of the mirror with arched back and upright tail to fend off the reflection he saw. I hid under the covers laughing while he jumped on top and tried to claw his way through the duvet.

Our cosy evenings on the sofa by the fireside became a thing of the past. Alvin came alive at night, usually around 8pm when we were settling down for the evening. He careered round the house jumping on seats and tables, fur on end, his big ears flattened to his head and his tail bushed out like an elaborate loo brush. Comically, sometimes he ran sideways until all co-ordination broke down, his rear legs overtook his front ones and his back end tumbled over his head.

During these mad outbursts his *coup de grace* was an airborne assault on me in which he launched himself at my face with claws unsheathed and teeth bared. As he grew, so did his arsenal and it became increasingly challenging to parry him away before he made contact. As a small kitten I swatted him away like a fly; at five months old I had to grab him and restrain him. To him it was all mock fighting, but I started to accumulate scars in my arms and face as a result of these encounters.

Alvin enjoyed "playing" with me, much more than he enjoyed playing with Stephanie. He reserved his affections for her and viewed me as a human scratch post. On many occasions, he clambered up my legs and back, often when I was on the phone, digging his talons in along the way and forcing me to apologise to the person on the other end of the line for my subsequent swearing.

My limbs started to resemble those of a self-harmer and people in the gym looked at me with a mixture of shock and pity when I wore shorts and a t-shirt.

The attacks were unprovoked. One night we were sitting in front of the television watching DIY SOS, a show that I was regularly emotionally hijacked by. As the big reveal unfolded at the end of the hour and Nick Knowles wheeled a disabled war veteran and his young family around their new, redesigned home, I began to fight back tears. Alvin looked at me, perplexed and slowly started to crawl onto my lap. It was a breakthrough moment. Could he really sense my heightened emotional state? Was he empathising? He was purring, and slowly he started to creep higher up my chest, as if to comfort me further. I reached out and stroked him gently. His little body was vibrating. I felt soothed. Alvin climbed higher until, amazingly, we were eye-to-eye. His expression, while impassive to anyone who didn't know him, was one of concern. I was sure he could sense my pain. He held me in his hypnotic gaze. I was transfixed. I felt a connection, as if two species divided by eons of evolution were somehow sharing a common bond of understanding.

Stephanie watched.

"He's looking into my soul," I whispered, awe-struck.

And then, with the speed and aggression of a striking cobra, he lunged forward and sunk his teeth into the tip of my nose.

I shrieked. Alvin clung on, his canines embedded firmly. I grabbed him and yanked until he let go. Blood started to drip from the wound. Alvin stood his ground, tail flicking, proud of his work. I cursed him and shuffled off to attend to another wound while Stephanie creased up in fits of laughter.

I spoke to cat-owning friends about his behaviour and the consensus seemed to be that it was a mix of youthful exuberance, boredom from being confined in the house, curiosity, boundary testing and jealousy, as cats protect the females in their groups and Alvin viewed Stephanie as his female.

He became increasingly brazen and daring in his incursions. As his claws strengthened he developed an incredible ability to climb. Bengals are a hybrid breed derived from crossing a domestic cat with an Asian leopard cat, which is a solitary, small wild cat native to Southeast Asia. Leopard cats are agile climbers and rest in trees. Alvin appeared to have inherited some of his ancestor's abilities. He scaled curtains easily, would always look to reach the best vantage point in a room and on one occasion I marvelled when I watched him scale the exposed brick wall in my office. His climbing skill allowed him new locations from which to launch attacks. One night, when I thought he'd left the room, I sidled up to Stephanie for a cuddle on the sofa. Alvin was waiting quietly behind the curtain above, his claws holding him in place. In a flash he launched himself at me like a feline Exocet missile. He went straight for the face again and managed to catch my cheek and forehead as he sailed past. The scars lasted a month.

Another night, when Stephanie was away, I was setting a fire in the fireplace and Alvin trotted over to have a look. He climbed on to the fire grill and stared up the chimney breast. I should have pulled him back but instead encouraged him.

"What's up there Alvin?" I said.

It was as if I'd given him permission and in an instant he bolted straight up the hole into soot-stained murk.

"Bugger," I hissed. Then: "Alvin, come down." I could hear him moving around but had no idea how far he'd got or whether he was stuck.

More urgently: "Alvin, come on." More movement. Soot dropped down onto the hearth. For a split second a dark thought crossed my mind. What if I lit the fire? I could say it was a terrible accident. But the truth of the matter was, despite my regular injuries and the obvious tension between me and my cat, I begrudgingly found his behaviour amusing, and at times even endearing, particularly when he got himself into mischievous scrapes. Very slowly he was beginning to get under my skin. If went out for the day, on my way home I started to think about him. He always trotted over to greet me and I couldn't help but be disarmed by his enthusiasm. I resisted and tried to remain nonchalant, but he could be unbearably cute when he wanted to be. I also found that the constant threat of ambush had heightened my reflexes and on occasion, I even enjoyed our 'play' sessions. I saw it as my duty to toughen Alvin up through play, so he had the skills to thrive when he was eventually allowed out of the house, much as an alpha male would do in the wild.

"Please come down Alvin," I pleaded. I heard shuffling and suddenly his soot-covered face peered from the gloom. Anyone else would have seen the impassive Alvin stare. I saw a naughty grin.

"Get down," I ordered, half stern, half laughing. It was impossible to be cross with him. Once more he disappeared into the gloom.

Eventually I coaxed him down with treats and then chased after him as he bolted off through the house, leaving a trail of soot on the floor and across the beige sofa, onto which I eventually pinned him down and wrapped him in a tea towel before taking him to the kitchen, where I washed him under the tap as he squirmed and yowled with indignation.

Each week brought a fresh challenge as Alvin learned new tricks. He mastered how to open drawers. He forced his paw into any that were left ajar and carefully jimmied them open wide enough to enable him to ransack them. But he only ever seemed to target my possessions, which reaffirmed my belief that he had a jealous vendetta against me. When he opened the key drawer, it was only my car key he found. I discovered it on the floor the following morning with the locking and unlocking buttons chewed off it. One morning when Stephanie was away on business, I was awoken by the sound of smashing glass. I thought the house was being burgled. When I went to see what had happened I discovered that Alvin had climbed to a high shelf in the lounge and knocked a framed picture to the floor. It was a portrait of me with Stephanie.

His behaviour became increasingly erratic and I turned to the internet for answers. Before we got Alvin I did very little research into his breed but, after I caught him trying to eat a box of paper clips, I logged on to the Bengal Cat Club website to discover whether his quirks were normal, or whether he had psychological issues.

Bengals, apparently, were bred to be pleasant and trustworthy family companions. I snorted and looked down at Alvin, who was busy trying to chew another twisted paperclip.

"Bengals are intelligent and athletic," it said. They were curious and playful, vocal, self-assured, confident and extremely energetic. On another site I discovered they were exuberant, excitable and got very attached to their owners, which could lead to jealousy. Another theorised that the character Tigger in Winne the Pooh was based on a Bengal. If all that was true, and if Alvin possessed all those characteristics (which I suspected he did), ostensibly, what we had done was home the feline equivalent of a child with ADHD who had eaten all the blue Smarties.

It became increasingly difficult to work in my office because Alvin moved in. Depending on what I was doing, I spent a lot of time in the office. Alvin's appearance coincided with a book project (I was ghost-writing a memoir for an Afghan war hero). After the interviewing stage this meant long days at the computer screen, writing and editing.

My office was my territory. It was the one room in the house where I had free reign. When I was writing books I transcribed the interviews and used them to build a subject index. The index, which often ran to 20 pages, was then used to build a chapter plan. I printed out the index and pinned it to the wall, which usually meant that at least one wall was full of sheets of lists of random phrases and numbers. This work involved a great deal of concentration and depending on deadlines, I usually set a target of 3,000 words a day, but could get 5,000 done at a push if I "pulled an all-nighter" and worked into the early hours. So when Alvin's bed arrived, along with his litter tray and toys, I was not thrilled. Initially I wanted to shut him out, but he just stood outside the door making a racket, so in the end I resigned to myself to his presence until the magic six-month deadline was up and he could go where he pleased. It became a period of incarceration for both of us, a fractious inter-species office share in which my co-worker was an imbecile who on occasions would crap in the corner.

I discovered that Alvin liked keyboards – specifically, my keyboard. On countless occasions I was sitting at my computer working when suddenly Alvin became bored and launched up my leg on to the desktop (my leg was his favourite route to any high point). Once there he ran across the keys, and I lost several pieces of work because he always managed to find the delete button. He also enjoyed chewing wires and pulling peripherals out of sockets at the back of the computer. In dark times I toyed with the idea of dabbing cat food on the main power lead in an effort to teach him a lesson.

Even the bathroom offered no sanctuary. The rule that cats hate water doesn't apply to Bengals. They love it. So whenever I managed to steal a bath or a shower with Stephanie, Alvin was there, eyeing me suspiciously and dipping his paw in the water.

He was omnipresent. He was in every room and, as I was mainly the one in the house, he followed me everywhere, constantly vying for attention, always wanting something. I did my best to accommodate him but found myself getting behind on work projects.

With a newfound knowledge of his breed, it was apparent that Alvin was getting bored of his confines and needed more stimulus. I tried as best as I could to play with him but he played rough. We played chase through the house and up and down the stairs as I tried to wear him out, particularly in the evenings in the vague hope that I might get a full night's sleep, as he had taken to waking us up as soon as it got light.

He particularly enjoyed hide and seek. We would take it in turns crouching behind furniture and jumping out at each other. I'd startle him, and he'd speed off, me in hot pursuit. Then, when I'd got him and playfully pinned him to the ground, he'd run off for me to chase. He usually waited under the bed and jumped out, claws extended.

Stephanie watched our games with bemusement.

"I thought you didn't like cats," she said.

"I don't. I'm just trying to burn off a bit of his energy, so we get some peace," I argued.

"You love him," she laughed.

Perhaps love was too strong a word, but I had to admit to myself that despite the headaches he caused, I was getting rather fond of him.

Cat bromance aside, we both looked forward to his freedom. Six months was a long time to be locked up with an idiot and he would often sit by the window and look wistfully into the garden, fascinated by the world beyond that was tantalisingly out of reach. Before he was allowed out there was one hurdle he would have to overcome, and I was conflicted about it. Alvin would need to be castrated – for a number of reasons. It was the responsible thing to do, it would stop him wandering off and it would apparently calm him down. While I was in agreement, as an intact male I also felt a primal sympathy and a sense that I was betraying him. Part of me admired his base wild male instincts and the clock was ticking down to a time when they would be blunted by a vet's scalpel. It might as well have been my hand flicking open his scrotum.

One night, not long before he was due his operation and subsequent freedom, I was alone with him in the lounge trying to relax while he had his usual evening frenzy. In a corner under a drawer unit I saw movement. When I looked, I saw a huge spider making its leisurely way along the skirting board. It was, without a lie, one of the largest spiders I've ever seen outside of a zoo. Its legs were covered in coarse hair and its abdomen was fat and juicy. Huge fangs protruded from its head. I don't mind spiders but this one made me shiver.

As I watched it, I hatched a plan. Alvin's distant cousins were supposed to be prolific hunters and so somewhere in his DNA, he should have had an instinct to hunt. He was oblivious to the arachnid behemoth that was lurking in the corner so I got on my hands and knees and slowly crawled towards it, so as not to startle it and send it scuttling off.

I quietly called Alvin and, perplexed, he sauntered over to see why I was on the floor. The spider was still.

"Look Alvin," I said, pointing at the black creature hunkered against the wall, "what's that?"

Alvin saw it and cautiously moved forward. The spider twitched. Alvin jumped slightly and made a noise I'd never heard before, like a vibrato meow. He went down on his haunches and the spider, sensing danger, made a break for it. Quick as a flash Alvin darted forward and patted it with a paw. The spider changed direction and Alvin let it run momentarily, then darted towards it and stopped it again. His every sinew and nerve was alive. The spider stopped, faced him and reared up, raising its front legs and exposing its fangs. I swear I heard it hiss.

Alvin swatted it with a paw and sent it skittering across the polished wooden floorboards. It got back to its feet (only seven by now as the blow had detached one, which was still twitching), and made a dash for cover. Alvin caught it again, enjoying the sport. I watched, half fascinated, half horrified. Like a voyeuristic onlooker at a road accident, I reached for my phone and snapped a picture of the battle as Alvin backed his adversary into a corner and it reared up again. Stephanie, who was away at the time and who was an arachnophobe, would be so proud, I thought to myself.

The battle between cat and spider raged for several minutes and Alvin could have been merciful and finished it long before it eventually ended. Instead he toyed with his prey in an almost orgasmic, psychotic state, revelling in its misery until the floor was strewn with spider legs and the spider was dead. When the fight was over, Alvin picked up the body and threw it around a bit before crunching down on it with his jaws. I shuddered and felt disgusted with myself for what I'd encouraged. Alvin, on the other hand, seemed very pleased with himself. I began to think that perhaps castration was not such a bad option after all. There was obviously testosterone flowing through his veins that was fuelling blood lust.

I walked over to Alvin and picked up the carcass he'd dropped on the floor. It was unrecognisable and oozing fluid. I threw it on the fire, where it sizzled and popped.

I sat back down on the sofa and Alvin jumped up next to me and sidled into my side. He seemed serene and at peace, the most satisfied I'd ever seen him. I felt uneasy at what I'd just witnessed. What kind of a monster had I unleashed? Alvin fell asleep by my side, purring, a twitching spider leg still hanging out the side of his mouth.

I knew then that I had to establish our positions in the house. Alvin needed to be controlled and I vowed to be the one to take him to the vet so that when he came round from the anaesthetic and realised something was terribly amiss in his nether regions, I would be there to remind him that I was the daddy, not him.

And yet I had to admit that my feelings were changing. Alvin was undoubtedly a character. He was a loveable rogue and rather than divide Stephanie and me, he brought us together. We were very close before, but Alvin provided another dimension to our home, like a feline cement that bonded us all together. We'd go out and find ourselves talking about him like parents talk about their kids. We'd recount things he'd done during the day to each other and ponder what he was getting up to while we were not there. Secretly, when I wasn't with him, I missed him. Something was happening to me and it made me feel quite uncomfortable. I had a cat, and I liked it.

CHAPTER FOUR
ENTENTE CORDIALE

On the day of Alvin's castration, I woke up feeling nervous and guilty. He had no idea what lay in store for him and was playing happily with a toy mouse when he was coaxed into the carrier that would take him to the vet. In a Judas-like betrayal, I threw a couple of meaty treats into the carrier and encouraged him inside, before closing the door behind him while he chewed greedily, completely ignorant. He looked at me through the bars – the Alvin stare was one of innocent puzzlement. In the car he meowed a few times but as the surgery was only a five-minute drive he didn't have time to get worked up. Once inside, he was full of curiosity when he was let out in the consulting room to be checked over, weighed and measured.

Alvin was a sociable cat. He had no choice, as our house was always full of people coming and going, so he was used to new faces.

When Stephanie first moved to "The South", one of the things she noticed was just how unfriendly people could be. She had moved away from a community where people talked to each other and left her close network of friends and family to be in a place where people avoided eye contact on public transport. When we chose Ashtead, we picked it as a location for two main reasons: it had a fishmonger's, and it was a village so had a community feel. Stephanie embraced the community and made friends easily. I had the usual southerner's wariness.

If we went for a walk, Stephanie would smile and say "hello" to strangers she passed. Many recoiled in horror.

"Stop it!" I hissed. "They will think you're mad." But my discomfort just made her do it more.

As a result of her chirpy disposition, we soon got to know all the neighbours and Stephanie made it clear that ours was an open house. Anyone was welcome to pop in. I just shook my head and explained that it wasn't the way we did things in the south. But secretly I enjoyed the fact that I could walk to the shop at the end of the road and talk to several people along the way.

Back in the surgery, Alvin played up to the young female vet, purred, nudged her with his head and behaved impecca-bly. He was flirting with her, totally unaware that within 30 minutes she'd be slicing open his scrotum to demasculate him. As she explained the details of the procedure I stood, crossed-legged, and looked down at our cat. At that moment, as he naively attempted to play with the vet, I felt a sudden rush of compassion. His innocence was heart-breaking. I worried about the effect the operation would have on his subsequent behaviour. He was undoubtedly a handful. He had come into our house and turned it upside down, destroyed much, caused injury and wreaked havoc, but begrudgingly I had started to see him as part of the family and every expletive-filled excla-mation I directed towards him when he broke something or playfully attacked someone was always backed with humour, I played the part of a curmudgeonly, reluctant owner, but I was actually starting to enjoy his crazy behaviour and he made me laugh. I could never get angry with him, no matter what he broke. Given a choice between this Alvin, and a neutered, lethargic Alvin who preferred to stay at home and be cuddled, I knew which option I would pick. Sterilising him seemed like a barbaric form of social engineering. Were we doing it for his sake or for ours?

"Will he be different when he comes home?" I asked.

The vet explained that the effects of castration differed from animal to animal but that it shouldn't affect personality. In most cases it reduced the need for cats to roam or to spray and also reduced aggression, which was a plus.

Still, my conscience tugged at me as Alvin was placed in his carrier and taken away to the back of the veterinary clinic. As he went we shared one last anxious glance through the bars of his cage. It was the last time I saw him in his natural intact state.

The operation was performed under general anaesthetic and the surgery kept Alvin in for most of the day to monitor him until he was recovered and had eaten. My initial plans to gloat and use his prone state to exert my place at the top of the hierarchy were the last thing on my mind when I drove to pick him up. I almost expected to find him wrapped in a shawl, knitting, having been stripped of his youthful male vigour.

"He's fine," said the vet nurse when she brought him out in his cage. "He's got a couple of stitches which need to come out in a few weeks. And keep an eye on him. If he keeps licking the wound it might mean there's an infection. Keep him inside until it's healed and the stitches are out. Apart from that there shouldn't be any problems."

I looked inside the carrier and Alvin looked up at me and meowed. I half expected the greeting to be delivered in a higher pitch. He seemed okay, if a little disorientated.

Back at home he was let out and wandered around the house, looking a bit lost and forlorn, rubbing against bits of furniture to lay his scent down. He seemed quiet and pensive when he sat down on his bed. He started grooming himself and then bent round to inspect his rear quarters. He sniffed suspiciously at his scrotum, then licked gently. He definitely knew there was something awry down there and he looked up at me with what I perceived to be alarm.

"Sorry mate," I shrugged. "It's for your own good, I promise."

Sadly, Alvin was unable to grasp the wider societal reasons why his testicles had to go. In the history of domestic cats, neutering is a fairly new phenomenon. Before veterinary advances made castration and spaying a safe procedure, euthanasia was the preferred method of population control. Today the British Veterinary Association "strongly supports the practice of neutering cats and dogs for preventing the birth of unwanted kittens and puppies and the perpetuation of genetic defects." It acknowledges that neutering is not a trivial procedure but says the welfare implications are outweighed by the benefits.

Removing the ability to reproduce in household cats that are allowed to wander is actually a necessity because, with their natural instincts and reproductive apparatus intact, they are prolific breeders. According to the feline welfare charity Cats Protection, which assists in neutering over 175,000 cats in the UK each year, one female can be responsible for 20,000 descendants in just five years. Female cats, or queens, can become sexually mature at four months and can have three litters a year. The average litter size varies between breeds but is usually between two and five kittens. The world's largest litter of domestic cats were born on the 7 August 1970 when a Burmese Siamese cross cat from Oxfordshire, UK, gave birth to 19 kittens, four of which were stillborn. Average for the type is between four and six.

Feral cat overpopulation puts a huge strain on shelters and welfare organisations. It often leads to euthanasia when animals cannot be rehomed. The problem became so acute in Belgium that a law requiring the compulsory neutering of nearly all the nation's cats was introduced and will apply nationwide by 2020, making it the first country in the world to require its citizens to mandatorily spay and castrate their felines. In 2018, there were two million cats in Belgium (and 11 million citizens) and a growing stray population which was bolstered by 30,000 cats abandoned each year. As a consequence, up to 13,000 cats were euthanised every 12 months. By comparison, in the UK around a quarter of the adult population owns a cat and charity Cats Protection estimates there are around 1.5 million feral cats, so we too have a sizable problem.

Belgium, incidentally, has a mixed relationship with cats. Kattenstoet, a festival held every three years in the town of Ypres, includes a three-hour cat parade and a witch burning re-enactment. It culminates with a ceremonial cat tossing from the belfry of the tower in the main square. Thankfully the cats aren't real any more (that practice stopped in 1817) and are stuffed toys instead. The tradition started in the Middle Ages, when the town jester would throw live cats to their deaths because the central market was overrun with feral felines. The ritual was supposed to chase away the evil spirits with which cats were said to be allied.

Cat tossing aside, more enlightened Belgians saw the potential of the feline populace in later years, and in 1879 some bright sparks in the city of Liège thought it would be a good idea to train a group of cats to deliver the mail. A unit of 37 postal delivery cats were trained to carry parcels in waterproof pouches around their necks. The scheme was developed by a resident named Mr Wegg and was supposed to help domestic servants in the town and outlying villages to stay in touch. The theory behind the scheme was that most cats lived in kitchens and would find their way back to their homes from outlying areas. The New York Times reported: "Unless the criminal class of dogs undertakes to waylay and rob the mail-cats, the messages will be delivered with rapidity and safety." The service was short-lived, however, as the cats tended to wander off wherever they wanted.

Newly neutered Alvin also missed his opportunity to become a mail cat, as his lack of gonads would theoretically stymy his urge to wander. His wounds healed quickly and my concerns about his personality proved baseless. In fact, the loss seemed to have the opposite effect on his libido. Before the surgery, he had begun to show an unnatural interest in soft toys. But only one type. Both the children had identical soft black-and-white spotted Dalmatian toys on their beds that were floppy, long and thin. Let's just say Alvin liked playing piggy-back with them. I assumed this little romance would end after his surgery, but in fact it intensified. Alvin would grab the toys with his teeth by the scruff of the neck and climb on top. It didn't matter which one, and he always had a creepy look of intent in his eye. If he was disturbed by Stephanie or me *in flagrante*, he looked guilty, dismounted and slunk off. We tried to hide them, but he sniffed them out. One day, we caught him with both of them. One was discarded carelessly in a crumpled heap at the side while we was atop the other, like some kind of twisted cat Caligula.

"What do you think he'd do if ever encountered a real Dalmatian?" I wondered.

He continued causing havoc with as much enthusiasm as he had done previously, much to my relief. And he was free to do it outside the house. It had been a long winter, both of us had been confined together indoors and when he took his first steps outside as spring approached, he revelled in the new and thrilling environment where a cacophony of sights, sounds and smells set his senses tingling. He was primed for adventure and I smiled as I watched him explore the garden. He never tired of chasing flies and would pin them down when he caught them, hold them in the grass and then leap after them again when he released them. Whenever I caught him with a bee, I freed it over the neighbour's fence, not because I was concerned about him getting stung – he had a protective layer of fur and would have to learn the rules of the natural world – but because I felt sorry for the bees. I had a slight niggling worry that he would get lost, but this was negated by his obvious delight at freedom.

Alvin had the benefit of a cat flap in the side of the conservatory that was unlocked during the day to allow him freedom, but locked at night as he was still small and unsure of his surroundings. As a consequence, most evenings as it started to get dark either Stephanie or I would have to stand out on the patio, calling for him. As he started to wander further afield and discover new and exciting places, he became less eager to come in for his "bedtime".

We lived in an area full of cat distractions. The front of the house was on a busy main road, but no one ever used the front door as we always went in from the back through the garden. Beyond the back-garden fence there was a small, quiet private access alley that the neighbouring houses backed on to as well. At the end of this was a quiet lane with a cycle café, Indian restaurant, hairdressers, sweet shop and fishmonger. All the neighbours owned pets. On one side we had guinea pigs and on the other two cat brothers named Julio and Fernando. They arrived around the same time as Alvin but only ventured outside after he did and were subsequently shy. Further along, another neighbour, Ben, owned a beautiful blue Chartreux cat named Duke who was easy going and mild mannered. John and Carole, who owned Dorking Fisheries, two dogs and a seldom-seen white and ginger cat, also lived nearby. On the other side of the alley there was a Grade 1 listed timber 16th-century cottage with immaculate gardens. Sarah, who lived there with her son Joseph, owned a vocal Irish water spaniel named Murphy. Sarah's garden seemed to be a popular thoroughfare for most of the cats in the area as it allowed them to roam without having to negotiate any roads.

As all the neighbours in our vicinity also used the back access alley to get to their properties, none of the cats ever ventured out to the main road, which seemed remarkable, and there were never any stories of cats being run over. Initially I was afraid that Alvin would wander in the wrong direction, but he never did and whenever the front door was opened or answered, we always took extra care to make sure he was shut away. In his mind, there was nothing of interest at the front of the house – just the unpleasant noise of cars.

Cats are supposed to be territorial and solitary, but Alvin was very sociable and hung around the back alleyway, greeting the neighbours and making his existence known. While there must have been a hierarchy between the animals in the neighbourhood, Alvin never came home with any injuries and we never heard any fights. In fact, endearingly, Alvin and Duke, who was large and muscular so presumably would have been the dominant male in the area, appeared to strike up a friendship. Alvin followed him around and often they'd sit in the sun together, seemingly happy to share the same territory. But while Duke rarely ventured into our garden, Alvin was happy to use everyone else's. When our immediate neighbour let her guinea pigs out in their run on the lawn, Alvin would scoot through the line of fir trees that acted as a boundary between our gardens, zip over the fence and sit by the chicken wire for hours, transfixed by the squeaking creatures inside. In the other direction he'd often wander up the stairs that led to Ben's door and push his way through Duke's cat flap to help himself to any food left in the kitchen. He was sneaky about these incursions and we only realised what was happening when Ben explained that he'd arrived home from work one day and had been making something to eat in the kitchen when, out of some unknown hiding place, Alvin had appeared and made a bolt for the catflap, which had been locked in the meantime. Alvin hit the catflap with such intent and velocity that it snapped out of its frame. Embarrassed, we apologised profusely and offered to buy a replacement.

Alvin had a way of introducing himself and, as a result, of introducing us to the community, which had a profound effect.

Neighbours we hadn't met before or spoken to would stop when they saw our cat, because he was striking and also stupidly friendly. Inevitably, we would start to chat. Initially, as a born-and-bred Londoner, I was suspicious and uncomfortable. But as we got to know more of the people around us, I started to relax into community life.

Alvin's circle of friends included some of the village's most colourful characters. The staff from the curry house who lived in flats a few properties along stopped to chat to him and several of the residents in a small development of flats and mews houses at the end of the alley knew him too. Unbeknown to me, one of them frequented the gym I was a member of. I discovered his soft spot for Alvin by accident one day when I made a faux pas on the gym floor. His name was Dave, and, at first sight, he was the type of man you would cross the road to avoid. With a shaved head, intense glare and thick-set muscular frame, he looked like a gangster from a Guy Ritchie movie. I had never noticed him before and was working out in the gym when I noticed a new piece of equipment hanging where the punch bag used to be. It was a heavy leather ball and, as no one was using it, I started to mess around with it.

"I didn't say you could use it, but help yourself," sniffed Dave as I attempted to punch the ball that was zipping around my head.

"There's other pieces of equipment," I told him. "This was free."

He bristled. What I didn't know was that the punch ball belonged to him. He'd brought it to the gym specially to train with and I'd barged in when he wasn't looking. He didn't look the kind of man who took kindly to having his boxing practice interrupted.

"It's mine actually, but like I said, use it if you want. You might want to stand a bit squarer and get your body behind the punches though," he advised, raising an eyebrow at my cack-handed technique. When I managed to connect, the ball rebounded back and glanced off the side of my head. Dave scoffed.

"Haven't I seen you somewhere?" he asked.

"I don't know, I've not been a member here for long," I answered as I clumsily tried to save face and duck out the way of the ball that was pinging around in front of me.

"You live in Ashtead don't you?"

When we realised we were neighbours, I stopped lashing out at the punch ball, took off the gloves I was wearing and introduced myself. I told him where I lived and he explained that he lived in one of the mews houses nearby.

"I've got a mate who lives on one of those houses near you. I don't know his name, it's a cat," he laughed. "Whenever I walk past, he always comes out to say hello and sometimes he'll follow me and stand outside my window. I pick him up and he'll butt against my head, he's a lovely little thing. He looks like a leopard."

"That's my cat," I laughed. "He's called Alvin. He's very friendly."

"Good name," said Dave.

I actually began to feel a tinge of pride when he talked about Alvin and explained that he didn't usually like cats but that Alvin was such a character, he couldn't help but like him.

"I know what you mean," I said. "I hate cats."

He looked at me, puzzled.

"I mean I used to hate cats, and generally I'm not fussed about them, but he's not like other cats. He's more like a human."

We both laughed and Dave nodded. It was true. Alvin wanted to be liked. He was sociable, outgoing and confident. He trotted out to greet the neighbours, made friends with the other cats and was fearless in his pursuit of attention. He also seemed to have an unusual knack of bringing out the best in people. Dave, as I discovered later, had a colourful past and had been involved in some scrapes with the law. He was certainly not a person you would want to get on the wrong side of. But when it came to Alvin, he was a complete softie.

As Alvin cemented his place in the community, he also had adventures. On one notable, bizarre occasion he even helped the authorities when they raided a flat above one of the shops. It was sunny weekday and Stephanie and I had taken a rare half hour in the afternoon to sit on the sunny veranda outside the cycle café for tea and cake. Usually we had lunch at our desks and were too busy to grab any down time in the days. Alvin was out somewhere, surveying his territory and enjoying the good weather. Suddenly a white van pulled off the main road and into the lane, where it came to an abrupt stop. Two black saloon cars followed. The side door of the van slid open, as did the car doors, and around 10 men and women in uniform jumped out and ran into our alleyway. The staff from the café came outside to see what was happening and we all stood, fascinated and shocked by what was unfolding. It was obvious that the raid was directed at a nearby property where several people lived, always coming and going.

We heard some shouting and, being the nosey journalist I am, I walked over the road to see what was going on. Several people were being held by the officials and questioned. Others had scarpered off through the mews houses at the top of the alley.

Then I caught sight of Alvin standing outside the open garage of a neighbour. He was looking in and meowing excitedly, the tip of his tail flicking from side to side. One of the officers also saw him and walked over. As he did he looked in the garage and saw someone hiding behind the car parked inside.

"Come on out, I can see you," the officer demanded. A young man, dressed in a t-shirt, shorts and flip-flops skulked out of the shadows. I looked at him apologetically. Alvin didn't mean to snitch on him, he just thought it was another game of hide and seek.

I picked him up and carried him over to the café where there was an audience watching the drama unfold.

"I think he'd better stay out the way," I said.

CHAPTER FIVE

KILLER INSTINCT

Alvin's affinity with his human neighbours, and his tolerance and openness with the cats in the area, did not extend to the local wildlife. As his first spring progressed the killing started, and I began to wonder if I'd unleashed a monster. This sounds dramatic, but his graduation from flies and spiders to warm-blooded mammals was fast and furious. Of course, to look at him, you would never know. Kittens are typically fully grown between nine and 12 months and as Alvin neared his first birthday, he remained long but slim, with small features and a handsome angular face. Once outside, his coat became browner as the Bengal markings came through and he grew into a striking cat. He looked cute and friendly, but, if you were a bird or a mouse, he was a deadly assassin.

The killing started innocently enough with a mouse; he brought his first blood proudly to the back door, dead and slightly chewed around the edges.

"Well done," I congratulated, unaware of the horrors that were to follow. Alvin played with his first catch for a bit, tossing the tiny carcass in the air like a toy. When he got bored of it I picked it up by the tail and threw it into a deep compost hole that the previous owners had dug in the flower-bed by the back door.

Alvin's catflap in the wooden conservatory behind the kitchen allowed him to come and go when the back kitchen door was open, but at night when it was locked, he was confined inside the house where he usually slept on the bed with us. However, as the summer arrived it started to get lighter earlier and at around four or five in the morning Alvin was up and ready to go out. He would then wake either Stephanie or me and one of us would have to go downstairs and let him out the kitchen door into the conservatory where he could wander off at his leisure. Inside the conservatory there were a few plants, a coffee table, a rocking chair and a tumble dryer. Alvin's bed was on top of the dryer and most days, when he'd been kicked out of the house, we would return home to the sight of his legs extended over the side of his bed. It was his favourite place.

He always brought his kills back, so in the morning, when we woke again after going back to sleep having let the cat out, there was usually something left outside. Most mornings one of us would open the conservatory door and outside there would be one, two or even three tiny carcasses. The maximum in one night was five, which was incredible considering that before Alvin arrived we'd never seen any mice in the house and never had any indications that there were so many in the vicinity.

His hunting ability was remarkable. As the weeks wore on, the bodies piled up and then the live animals started to arrive. It began one morning when I heard Alvin in a state of excitement in the conservatory running around the tumble dryer. He was trying to get at something behind it.

"What is it?" I asked him, but had a good idea what the answer was. I pulled the unit away from the wall a few inches and saw a terrified mouse huddled underneath. I called Stephanie and asked her to take Alvin indoors and shut him away. When he was secured, I opened the conservatory door, pulled the tumble dryer away completely and shooed the grateful rodent out. It was vermin, but I doubted very much that it would come anywhere near the house again. Once I was sure it was a safe distance away, Alvin was released and bolted out. He quickly sniffed around the conservatory, realised I'd foiled his fun, fixed me with an Alvin stare which said: "You bastard," then ran off outside to track his prey. I assume it survived because there was no more bloodshed that day.

Alvin's natural hunting instincts were obviously inherent. I'd never shown him how to stalk and catch a mouse and he hadn't been with his feline parents long enough to learn from them. Some cats hunt, others are too lazy, but generally, according to experts, too few generations have passed since cats were primarily kept as pest controllers for their instincts to have become totally blunted. Most modern moggies do not need to find prey to eat, as they get all the nutrition they need from their owners, but still they are hardwired to hunt. This was evident when Alvin was on the prowl. I could practically see every fibre of muscle twitching and every synapse firing as he focused intensely on the hunt. He came alive when he had prey. Sometimes he'd keep a mouse for hours, toying with it on the lawn. The compost pit became a macabre mass grave as the tiny bodies piled up. Each morning I guiltily disposed of the evidence and tried to hide it from the neighbour, who had a bird table in the middle of her garden which I became increasingly alarmed about. One morning she caught me performing another burial and threw an accusing look over the fence before taking her guinea pigs inside to safety.

To the outside world, Alvin was still the same adorable little character he had always been but I was privy to another, monstrous side of his personality. Everyone loved him. He trotted to the coffee shop around the corner and let himself in to most of the neighbours' houses. But in the early hours of the morning, as the world was slowly waking up, he stalked the neighbourhood like a feline Patrick Bateman, possessed of a blood lust I struggled to fathom.

Along with the horror came the guilt. As his reluctant owner, I felt complicit in the catmaggedon. I watched Springwatch through my fingers and Chris Packham's enthusiasm for songbirds filled me with sadness.

I could almost deal with the guilt of all those tiny mice souls, but when I noticed a male and female blackbird collecting twigs for a nest, and then, a few weeks later, making sorties for worms and grubs to feed their young, I was filled with dread. They had obviously nested nearby and something told me they were in mortal danger. To make matters worse, they made little effort to hide their presence in the area and hopped around our lawn most days singing, as Alvin watched intently before slinking off in the direction they headed, looking for an easy kill. It didn't take long.

He struck in daylight. I heard the commotion outside first. I was in the office and suddenly heard the shrill chirps of alarm as both male and female birds tried to distract Alvin from his prey. It was alive and in the conservatory. A fully feathered fledgling that he'd most likely snatched as it made its first tentative steps outside the nest. Immediately I grabbed him and shut him inside where he watched from a window, muscles twitching. The conservatory was full of black feathers but the bird could flap its wings and walk so I let it outside and it managed to fly a few feet before hiding under the fir trees.

I had read that if a fledgling could fly then the best course of action was to leave it, as the parents would feed it until it was strong enough to get to the safety of a branch or roost somewhere. I kept an eye on it and the parents hung around dutifully. Alvin was confined indoors for the rest of the day and at some point the bird must have got away because by the late afternoon it had gone, as had the parents.

Fledgling season is a particularly dangerous time for young birds as underneath the nest there will often be a cat waiting for stragglers. I told Alvin off for his actions, scolding him and telling him firmly that no, birds were out of bounds, but I couldn't be genuinely angry with him, how was he to distinguish between acceptable and unacceptable prey? I thought back to that first night in the lounge when I had encouraged him to kill the spider. As a fully-grown adult all my chickens (or blackbirds in this case) had come home to roost. Unfortunately, I feared most of them would end up torn apart on the lawn. A full bowl of Eukanuba and regular titbits did little to quell his appetite for flesh, and several more birds followed. He kept every one alive, brought them to the conservatory, and we managed to shut him away and get them to safety. Each one left me wracked with guilt.

I went online and looked for answers. Alvin was microchipped and we had tried to put collars on him when he was young, but he just pulled them off so we didn't bother any more. Now though, in order to hold back the tide of death, I started to order every device I could find. First, I started with a collar and bell. It was a struggle to get it on him and once it was secure he spent half an hour scratching and rubbing himself against furniture to get off. When he finally gave up he trotted off up the garden path, his collar tinkling like Noddy's hat. He looked totally fed up.

The following morning, I went downstairs and opened the kitchen door. Alvin was waiting for his breakfast as usual, minus the collar. Two days later, after a trip to Pets At Home, we tried a more secure collar (with an emergency release clip to stop him hanging himself). It lasted three days. I then discovered a bizarre neon bib on Ebay that was supposed to be the feline equivalent of a fluorescent safety vest and alert anyone and anything to the whereabouts of the wearer. The idea was good, but the application was lacking, and Alvin managed to get out of it in minutes. I did some research and read that hair scrunchies worn as Edwardian-style ruffs were effective. We fought as I tried to get one over Alvin's head. He won. It seemed there was no way to curtail his instincts.

Several weeks later the blackbirds were back with a second brood, as often happens. Alvin struck twice more, but rather than risk his prey/toy escaping the conservatory, he brought them into the house. Both times we were able to save the birds, which left blood and feathers all over the house. The second time, the thoroughly enraged parents followed and swooped through the house, squawking and dive-bombing the cat. It was complete chaos. Stephanie and I ducked through the forays and managed to get the poor youngster back outside.

His hunting wasn't restricted to the great outdoors. A lover of ladders, he made it his mission to get into the loft whenever the loft ladder was pulled down – particularly when birds nested in it and he could hear the cheeps of hatchlings above his place on our bed. He would sit on the duvet, ears twitching in spasms, tormented by the birdsong. Any attempt to get up to the loft turned into a race. As soon as Alvin heard the hatch open and the ladder extend, he raced to the upstairs hallway from wherever he was and leapt at the bottom rungs as soon as they were low enough. He managed to scale two thirds of the ladder before I grabbed him and he held on stubbornly with his claws and continued to try to pull himself up before I extracted him and shut him in a room. If he ever got up there I feared a bloodbath of birds and worried that in his frenzy he was likely to plunge through the gap in the eaves where the birds got in. Alvin got good at ladders and managed to get to the loft only once, thankfully several months after the birds had gone. He made straight for the corner where the nest had been and poked around with a disappointed look on his face.

He even became adept at ambushing humans, which was a regular hazard for anyone venturing down the garden path. The attacks were only ever meant to be playful, as Alvin didn't realise that his claws could cause damage, but on one occasion his exuberance sent a neighbour to hospital. Stephanie and I had booked a long weekend away and, rather than take Alvin to a cattery, we arranged for neighbours to pop in and feed him on a rota. Occasionally we'd been away for one or two nights, and Alvin was always pleased to see us when we returned, but was fine to be left on his own as long as his food and water were topped up. He was used to sleeping in the conservatory and there were plenty of neighbours around and people passing to keep him company.

We had been away for a night when Stephanie texted our friend Sarah, who owned Murphy the dog and was one of the neighbours on "Alvin duty", to ask how he was.

"He's fine," Sarah replied, "but he attacked me and I've been in A&E."

We were horrified and called her straight away. What on earth had he done to put a neighbour in hospital? I recalled the story of Shiny, a black moggy in the Cornish village of Little Treviscoe, which had terrorised residents and their pets and made homeowners so fearful that they hid behind locked doors and armed themselves with hoses and mugs of hot tea whenever they saw him prowling. He had been reported five times for violent behaviour, but police were powerless to act because laws designed to deal with dangerous dogs did not apply to cats. According to reports, in 2013 Shiny attacked a 90-year-old woman and put another victim in hospital after she received cuts and bruises from him. Surely Alvin hadn't done something similar? He was spirited, but he wasn't homicidal (unless you were a mouse).

Stephanie listened to Sarah with a worried look on her face.

"I'm so sorry," she kept repeating. "Can I do anything?"

"What if Sarah reports him and he has to be put to sleep?" I worried.

Stephanie hung up and shook her head.

"What? What's he done?" I asked.

"He jumped out at her from under the trees. She was wearing shorts and he caught her leg. She didn't need stitches but had a tetanus jab as a precaution."

"Oh God, is she okay?"

Thankfully she was, and although the scratch was quite deep and had bled profusely, there was no lasting damage. We surmised that perhaps Alvin had smelled Murphy on her and got over-excited. If anything, he was probably being over-friendly, and had never grown big enough to be a threat to anything other than birds and mice. The incident was treated light-heartedly and, to warn the other cat-owning neighbours of his new fearsome reputation, we changed the name of our Wifi network to "our cat is harder than yours", which flashed up on their phones and devices whenever they went to log in to their own networks.

***

In the meantime, at a loss over how to handle the constant carnage, I turned to a friend who knew all about the killing fields of spring in the suburbs. Simon Cowell ran the Wildlife Aid Foundation in Leatherhead, which dealt with 20,000 wildlife emergencies a year. Cats were his nemesis, particularly in the spring, when there was often a queue of people in the reception of the rescue centre he ran, holding shoe boxes with injured birds inside, each with missing feathers and tiny cat-tooth sized puncture wounds about their bodies.

"This time of year is always particularly bad because birds are coming out of the nest and are not very strong flyers, so they hop around on the ground where cats get to them easily," huffed Simon, as we sat in his office discussing the problem. He confirmed what I already knew, that if a cat owner manages to save a bird, the best outcome is for it to get back to its parents, who will often feed it somewhere safe on the ground for several days. However, this is only beneficial if the stranded bird is uninjured, because even a playful nip can prove fatal.

"Cats have so much bacteria on their teeth that a small bite can lead to infection and death. If we get a call from someone who has a cat attack victim of any species, the first thing we need to know is if there is any injury. If the skin has been broken, the risks are high and we would have to give the patient a course of antibiotics to be on the safe side," he explained.

For me, this was particularly hard to hear, as on the occasions I chased injured and terrified birds – or presents, as some cat owners call them – around the house and out to safety, I breathed a sigh of relief, unaware that they likely ended their days in a shivering fever of sepsis.

Simon recommended a collar with a bell on it. But we'd already tried that. Other places I looked for advice recommended keeping cats indoors before sunset and sunrise when birds are vulnerable, greasing bird table legs with Vaseline to stop cats climbing up them, and erecting a cat-containing electric fence linked to a special collar which would deliver a small electric shock when the cat got too near to the fence boundary.

Of course, Alvin, and every other hunting cat, could not be blamed for expressing his natural behaviour, and on a national scale, the figures are huge. According to the Mammal Society, cats in the UK catch up to 275 million prey animals each year, which includes 55 million birds. That was just the number known to have been caught – it excluded the animals that were caught but not taken home, or that escaped but subsequently died. The most frequently caught birds were house sparrows, blue tits, blackbirds and starlings.

In my research I did find a surprising crumb of comfort, however. While the numbers seem huge, there is no conclusive evidence to prove that cat predation has an impact on bird populations. Millions of birds die naturally each year, and cats tend to take the weak or sickly ones that would most likely perish in the wild anyway. The source of the information was the RSPB, which I assumed would have been anti-cat. But, in a measured statement, the organisation admitted the death toll is large but asserted that "there is no clear scientific evidence that such mortality is causing bird populations to decline."

"We also know that of the millions of baby birds hatched each year, most will die before they reach breeding age. This is also quite natural, and each pair needs only to rear two young that survive to breeding age to replace themselves and maintain the population. It is likely that most of the birds killed by cats would have died anyway from other causes before the next breeding season, so cats are unlikely to have a major impact on populations. If their predation was additional to these other causes of mortality, this might have a serious impact on bird populations," the statement read.

In fact, the bird species that have undergone the most serious population declines in the UK, such as skylarks, tree sparrows and corn buntings, rarely encounter cats, so they can't be blamed for their decline. Research shows that the real culprits are habitat change or loss, particularly on farmland.

So, while it was uncomfortable to witness, Alvin's spring killing spree was at least not contributing to a wider decline in numbers. And the more I investigated, the more I realised that while the concerns of wildlife lovers are completely legitimate, cats shouldn't be treated as pariahs. Humans have chosen to domesticate cats, and in so doing have invited a predator into households and gardens. While much can be done to quell the feline desire for flesh by feeding and disrupting hunting behaviour, cats are "hypercarnivores" or "obligate carnivores". This means they have to eat meat by necessity and they have a higher protein requirement than any other domestic mammals because, over millions of years of evolution, they lost the ability to digest plants. They are programmed to prey on small creatures. Unlike humans, who are omnivores and can get most of their energy from carbohydrates, cats get theirs from protein. They are not the only creatures with a hard-wired thirst for flesh: mink, seals, hawks, crocodiles and most amphibians are also obligate carnivores. This evolutionary digestive quirk means that through their ancestral diet, cats have lost the ability to make certain compounds and vitamins with their own body, because the meat they eat already contains them. Why bother evolving the ability to make vitamin A from plant-based beta-carotene as humans do, when the animal you are consuming has already done it for you? The commonly held conception that cats are lazy even applies to their digestive system!

Cats also need a range of different nutrients including B vitamins niacin and thiamine and the amino acid taurine, which humans make naturally but which cats cannot. All of these are found in abundance in meat.

Because of their highly selective dietary requirements, cats can appear to be fussy eaters. Alvin would turn his nose up at a range of foods he was presented with, or happily eat one type exclusively for months, and then inexplicably go off it in an instant. I discovered that this was because cats' tastebuds have evolved to suit their diet. They cannot taste sugars, but can distinguish different taste profiles in meats that we would not detect. To them, some meat is sweeter than others, and some is bitter. Cats also have shorter digestive tracts than most mammals in relation to their body size, as they do not need the long gut and bacteria required for breaking down plant matter.

For all these reasons, Alvin's hunting prowess was a natural reaction to his most basic survival instincts. Even though there was a full bowl of food for him indoors at any time, his desire to hunt was programmed into him through millions of years of evolution. He could not switch off his predatory predisposition.

Eventually we put him under curfew and kept him inside early in the morning and at dusk, when birds are most vulnerable – and it seemed to do the trick, as did a diet fortified with more titbits of raw meat, which seemed to satisfy the blood lust. The mice continued to pile up in the death pit, but the birds stopped. One morning I was staggered to find a hedgehog carcass in the garden. Alvin was standing by its side looking pleased with himself. Through my connections with Simon and The Wildlife Aid Foundation I knew that hedgehog populations were in a parlous state in the UK and that they were protected. I also knew that the likelihood of Alvin having killed the hedgehog himself was remote. Dogs are known to attack them, but cats will investigate and then leave them alone. My suspicions were confirmed on closer inspection, when it became apparent that the flat carcass was old. The hedgehog probably died in a road accident and Alvin had discovered it somewhere and dragged it back as a trophy to show me. It was his macabre show-and-tell.

As spring turned to summer, I stood in the garden early one morning, another dead mouse held gingerly by the tail between my fingers, and Alvin stood next to me looking up. His wide-eyed, blank stare was saying: "that's for you, Daddy." I looked down at him and sighed. In his language, the mice were offerings. I didn't enjoy cleaning up the bodies and would rather they didn't appear at all, but he was doing what he was designed to do, and skilfully. He was a marvel of evolution and, despite my former reservations, we had reached a mutual understanding about our respective places in the household. I was becoming rather fond of him and I realised that after his initial jealous episodes, he was becoming rather fond of me too.

CHAPTER SIX

MOGGY VS DOGGY

As summer turned to autumn, Alvin swapped nights out for cosy nights in by the fire and snuggled up on the sofa between Stephanie and me, perfectly happy and content. While I still jokingly maintained that I didn't feel any affection for him, the reality was quite the opposite and I looked forward to his company. With all the skill of a seasoned hunter, he'd broken down my reservations and captured my affections and those of most of the people he came into contact with.

One night, when Stephanie was away for work, she called for a chat and we made idle conversation.

"Where's Alvin?" she asked.

"He's here on the sofa. We're watching a film, the fire's going and we've had sprats for tea."

I suddenly realised what I must have sounded like.

"Sprats? For tea? With the cat?" laughed Stephanie. "You've turned into a spinster from the 1950s."

It was true. That morning I'd specifically gone into the fishmongers after seeing the tiny fresh fish in the window. My mum used to cook them for tea on a Sunday. For some reason Sunday supper at the Hardings' always seemed to consist of something gleaned from a post-war ration cook book and along with sprats I also remember pig's trotters with pickle, tripe and onion, hearts and eels. At the sight of the sprats I was overcome with nostalgia and went in to buy several handfuls of the silvery fish, not because I was keen to eat them (although lightly seasoned, dusted with flour, fried and eaten whole they were delicious), but because I thought to myself: "Alvin will love these!"

"I have, haven't I," I laughed. "What's happening to me?"

Cats are agile creatures and it turned out that Alvin's agility was emotional as well as physical. He was always the centre of attention. When we had friends over for a garden party, Alvin didn't slink off somewhere quiet – he was always there, acting like the guest of honour, walking across the table at dinner parties, holding court on the armchair. He loved people and company.

The children adored him and he became particularly fond of Lucas. He could often be found on my son's bed, mainly because on the whole Lucas ignored him, whereas Millie tended to pick him up and cuddle him, which sometimes he enjoyed and other times barely tolerated. His relationship with Lucas was similar to that between brothers, with Alvin often tormenting his older human pseudo-sibling. One summer afternoon the children were in the garden under the apple tree putting together a rigid cardboard model of a shark that had been at the back of a drawer somewhere waiting to be built since Christmas. Alvin was in one of his favourite hiding places behind the line of fir trees. As the children neared completion of the rather technical puzzle, he leapt out onto it, obliterating their careful work and snapping a key piece. They taped it up and started again, only for a repeat attack. Eventually the model was abandoned, and Alvin was left to destroy it completely. Perhaps something about the fishy shape had caught his interest. The kids accepted his playfulness in the manner it was intended and found his behaviour as funny as everyone else did.

Alvin wasn't just a pet, he was a companion and, dare I say it, even a sort of friend. Working from home could be a lonely business, particularly given the long hours chained to a desk. And as the weather turned, for much of the day, Alvin stayed in the office, in his bed on top of the filing cabinet. He was one of the fixtures, looking down at me, judging me when I procrastinated, I imagined.

I had another ghost-writing project on the go, this time writing the memoirs of a former fugitive who evaded capture for over 20 years after he stole the Securicor van he was driving. The work meant regular trips to the south coast for the interviewing part of the job, and then long days in the office writing. On the days I was away I looked forward to getting home to see Stephanie and Alvin and the children if they were staying and on the days I was indoors Alvin was my companion. Stephanie would sometimes work in the office with me, but her business was growing and often she was out in London or away in other parts of the country. At home I tried to stick to a routine. In the mornings I would get to the gym early, around 6.30am. I'd spend an hour there, then come home and try to be at the desk working for 8.30am. Often, particularly when deadlines loomed and I was stressed about finishing the work on time, I would suffer insomnia and, in the early hours, creep down to the office to start work. Alvin would come with me and keep me company.

There are points in my cat journey that I can revisit and realise that I was falling under the feline spell. Pet owners will recognise the signs. I started to look forward to seeing him when I'd been out. I started calling him by pet names (Fella, Little Man, Big Ears). I took photos of him for no reason other than because he looked handsome. I showed those photos to friends (who thought I was going mad, particularly my hard-bitten cynical journalist friends).

"You need to get a life," they'd say.

Or: "Are you feeling okay? It's just a cat!"

When eyebrows were raised I found myself defensive. Should men really have cats? I justified myself by telling people: "He's not like a cat. He's more like a dog," as if that made it okay, because it seemed to me that dogs had managed to bag all the noble qualities that humans hold dear in companions, such as loyalty, faithfulness, sociability and playfulness, while cats were associated with the less desirable characteristics of detachment, laziness and stubbornness.

This shouldn't come as a surprise, however, when you consider that dogs have had 5,000 more years to develop bonds with humans than cats have. The first dogs are thought to have been domesticated in Europe 15,000 years ago, while the first cats are believed to have been domesticated 10,000 years ago. Studies indicate that the first domestication of wildcats took place in the Middle East, in the region known as the "cradle of civilisation", or Fertile Crescent, which stretched from the Nile in Egypt through Iraq, Syria, Lebanon, Cyprus, Jordan, Palestine and Israel. For many years it was believed that the ancient Egyptians were the first society to domesticate cats much later, around 3,600 years ago. Cats were depicted in Egyptian art, which suggests that they were valued for their role as pest controllers and as companions. Cats were also associated with religion and were treated with sacred respect. Bastet, the goddess of the home, cats, and fertility, was depicted either as a cat or as a woman with the head of a cat. When an Egyptian pet cat died, all the members of the family shaved off their eyebrows to mourn it and treasured cats were given the highest honour when they died and were mummified. Unfortunately for the cats of Egypt, this reverence also led to them becoming favoured sacrificial animals, of which the Egyptians had many. In fact, they were slaughtered on an industrial scale and bred specifically in catteries attached to temples so they could be offered up to the Gods and mummified.

However, the traditional view that the feline-loving/massacring Pharaohs gave the world the pet moggy was challenged by later genetic and archaeological evidence, which indicated that cats and people go back much further. First, in 2000, DNA analysis carried out by Dr Carlos Driscoll, WWF Chair of Conservation Genetics, pinpointed the direct wild descendent of every modern-day pet cat. His analysis showed that all domestic cats descended from one type of wildcat, *Felis silvestris lybica*, otherwise known variously as the Middle Eastern, Near Eastern or African wildcat and native to parts of the Fertile Crescent. Then, in 2004, archaeologists from the National Museum of Natural History in Paris discovered the earliest evidence of humans keeping cats as pets when they uncovered human remains buried with an eight-month-old cat in a shallow grave in Cyprus. The remains were 9,500 years old and arranged in such a way that suggested the cat had been buried with the human on purpose. It was also known that cats were not native to Cyprus and so must have been taken over to the island on boats, most likely from the adjacent Levantine coast, where African wildcats lived. During the period in question, the Natufian people were establishing agricultural settlements in the region. Natufians were sedentary hunter-gatherers who lived between about 12,500 and 10,200 years ago and are regarded as the first farmers. They collected wild grain that was so bountiful they needed to build stores to keep the surplus in. Archaeological digs have uncovered evidence to show that these grain stores were plagued by another visitor, *mus musculus*, the house mouse. Increasing numbers of mice would have attracted predators to the settlements and the most effective of these, the wildcat, would have stayed and most likely have been tolerated and even welcomed by humans. Fittingly, throughout their respective histories, cats and mice have been locked together in an eons-old conflict as enduring as an eternal *Tom and Jerry* cartoon, neither ever winning or losing.

The more I read up on the history of how cats became pets, the more I saw the links between the story of pet cats and the story of Alvin and me. He too had worked his magic on me the same way his entire species had worked their magic on mankind, first impressing as pest controllers and then as companions. Having a cat, I decided, was pretty cool. I was a convert.

Everyone gets pets for different reasons. Some people love animals and can't image a home without them in it. Some collect small menageries of pets. For others, pet owning becomes a family tradition passed down through generations. Some people are cajoled into buying a rabbit, puppy or kitten by their children whose promises to look after it usually fade after a couple of months. Others are lonely and just want some company. I came from a fairly unique perspective in that I never wanted a pet so I was philosophical about pet ownership. I realised that we kid ourselves that we are enriching the animal's life. The truth is that we keep pets for our own selfish reasons, not because they want to come and live with us. Alvin didn't choose me – if he had free choice, he would have stayed with his mother for a few more months and then wandered off to make his own life. We coerced him into our lives and although he seemed happy enough, I couldn't quite come to terms with the romanticised notion that he was a family member on equal terms with everyone else. He was a cat, not a human. The reality, as I saw it, was that he was half-interloper, half-Stockholm-syndrome-suffering kidnap victim.

As I researched articles about our links with our pets, I came across a little-known wartime story that seemed to illustrate my point that under the right circumstances the façade that pets are equal members of our families soon crumbles. On the eve of the outbreak of war in 1939, pet owners, particularly those in areas at risk of air raids, were advised to take their household animals to the country, or, if they could not be placed in the care of neighbours, to have them humanely destroyed. A government pamphlet advised that pets would not be allowed in air raid shelters and gave advice on humane methods to destroy Fido and Tiddles. On page two of the pamphlet, there was an advert for a captive bolt pistol which stated: "The Cash Captive Bolt Pistol provides the speediest, most efficient and reliable means of destroying any animal, including horses, cats and any size of dogs." Families, faced with the prospect of rationing and unimaginable hardship, made the false assumption that killing their pets was patriotic and humane. There was also concern that in any aerial mass poison-gas attacks on British cities, pets would become hysterical and run wild through streets contaminated by mustard gas.

The day Hitler invaded Poland there was panic as people either threw their pets out of their blacked-out homes or took them to vets or animal welfare organisations to be destroyed. In the first week of war it was estimated that up to 750,000 family pets were destroyed. Even London Zoo joined in and put down animals including snakes, a manatee, fruit bats, seven Nile crocodiles and two lion cubs. All were "destroyed owing to war conditions".

Many of those unfortunate pet owners would have agreed that their loyal pets were one of the family, and there is no doubt that the decision to put them down would have been agonising. But it's hard to imagine a similar response if the advice was to euthanise elderly human members of the family to help the war effort, or children who might use up vital rations.

Pets live in our homes and rely on us, and in return we take what we want from them. Alvin's position in our home was like the Isle of Man's position in relation to the UK. He was dependent, but he had no real voting rights. I liked him a lot, but I still didn't love him and certainly could never envisage feeling the same way about him that I felt about Stephanie or my kids. Some people might have accused me of being cold hearted, but it was honesty. Perhaps it's a harsh thought experiment, but if you were on a plane with your family and your cat or dog and plane was going down and you were one parachute short, I bet I know who would get the bum deal.

However, I could appreciate Alvin and more specifically I could appreciate the advantages of being a cat owner. For example, there was nothing more satisfying than looking out the window at a dog owner hunkered against the frost and rain, trudging along behind a mutt, carrying a little warm plastic bag of freshly laid turd. I would smile smugly to myself, open the back door and kick out Alvin, happy in the knowledge that my independent animal would go and defecate in someone else's garden while I stayed in the warm. No other scenario better illustrated the one immutable truth of animal ownership that I had learned. Cats were better than dogs, no contest. They were more convenient, they smelled less, they were cleaner, cleverer and cheaper.

"But my dog loves me unconditionally," dog-lovers would say as they stooped down to handle another parcel of excrement. They missed the point, and confused stifling canine neediness for adoration while failing to understand that a cat's casual detachment is what made it so cool. Alvin was the perfect pet to fit into our lifestyle. For two working people with busy lives, he was ideal. He required little maintenance, was a bundle of fun and kept the mice population in check.

We still had those discussions.

"You love him," Stephanie prodded. "You worry about him when we are away and you can't wait to see him."

"I admit, I'm fond of him, and he's fond of me," I conceded. "But it's a relationship of convenience and while we both derive pleasure from each other's company, it's a leap of faith to interpret that as love."

I said this with tongue firmly in cheek while I was feeding him cat treats that I'd been down the pet shop and bought him.

CHAPTER SEVEN
YOU'VE LOST THAT LOVING FELINE

Christmas came and went and I refused to buy Alvin a present, arguing rightly that cats don't observe religious festivals. But I was persuaded to buy Stephanie a present from him and write a card. I bought the card from Scribbler, a shop famed for its selection of obscene and offensive gifts. The card had a photograph of a bored-looking cat on the front over the words: "Please tell me more about your gluten-free diet."

Inside I wrote: "Dear Keeper. It's all very well celebrating Jesus's birthday, but look what you did to him later. You humans disgust me. Kind regards, Alvin (the cat)."

From then on, disgruntled cat greetings cards, filled with grumpy and objectionable messages, became a custom on special occasions.

On Christmas Day, as I predicted, Alvin, who was 18 months old, was uninterested in his presents, particularly the Elf outfit he had been bought. But he did perk up when the treats came out and enjoyed playing with the wrapping paper more than he enjoyed playing with the toys he'd been given.

In January, we had some work done in the garden in preparation for a cabin that was due to be built there and used as an office for Stephanie's expanding business. The work involved some major re-landscaping. The fir trees came out and the beds at the end of the garden and a sizeable patch of lawn were replaced by a shingle terrace, which I thought Alvin might view as a large litter tray. A few weeks later the cabin arrived. The changes to the garden didn't seem to faze Alvin, who wasn't keen on the machinery but made friends with the gardener who did the job.

Around the same time, I noticed a new feline face in the neighbourhood. A small, thin, silver-and-black striped cat had started to lurk around the back of the houses where Alvin patrolled and had apprehensively ventured a few feet into our garden on a couple of occasions. It wore a sparkly pink collar so I assumed it was a female. On the few occasions our paths crossed and when I got near to her, she backed off nervously. She had a much rounder face than Alvin's angular features and big, wide yellow eyes that made her look permanently surprised. She was young and was most likely experiencing her first weeks outside, exploring her new territory and finding her place in the local pecking order. Given her size and skittishness, I surmised she'd be at the bottom of the territorial rung and on occasion I started to hear wailing and hissing beyond the back gate, which was an indication that the cat politics in the area were shifting.

Our home improvements continued and in early February we had a new front door fitted, replacing the old wooden one that let in drafts and the noise of traffic on the main road outside. The morning started the same as many others. As had happened through most of the winter, Alvin had decided to stay in overnight and scratched at the carpet at 4am to wake one of us up so he could be let out. Like most cats he was at his liveliest just before dawn and dusk.

"Your turn," I mumbled, as Alvin brushed himself against my hand.

Stephanie got up and he followed her downstairs, where he stopped off for a few mouthfuls of food before heading out the back door into the conservatory and through the cat flap into the early morning gloom and freedom. If I'd have known what was going to happen, I would have made more of an effort to say goodbye. But it was just another normal early-hours interruption and I rolled over and went back to sleep, glad that Stephanie had got up instead of me.

Alvin didn't keep to routines and would regularly disappear for long periods of the day. Twice he'd stayed away overnight, once for two nights. On both occasions, when I opened the back door and saw that his legs weren't poking out over the side of his bed like they usually were in the morning, I felt a pang of panic and had to tell myself that he was a cat and that's what cats do. Each time he came back and I was relieved to see him. I always asked where he'd been, but he never told me.

At around 9am the door fitter arrived and parked his van at the back of the house. Before he started his work, I gave him some instructions.

"We've got a cat who comes in and out of the house. Can you keep an eye out for him because I don't want him going out the front door. Don't leave it open if you can help it please."

When Alvin showed up, I planned to shut him in the office with me for the day while the door was being fitted.

As the day wore on, the fitter became increasingly fraught and was faced with a series of problems. And at a couple of junctures during the day I also noticed that he'd left the door open and asked him to remember to keep it closed. In the end, what we had assumed would be a routine job turned into an epic all-day task and at the end of it, a hole had somehow been punched right through the hallway wall into the lounge, scattering bits of brickwork and plaster over the sofa and floor. As the fitter was clearing up the mess, I absent-mindedly asked him if he'd seen the cat. He said he hadn't. By the time the whole debacle was over it was early evening before Stephanie and I sat down for dinner.

"Have you seen Alvin?" Stephanie asked.

I frowned.

"I don't think so."

I cast my mind back over the day and couldn't recall whether he'd been in the house or not. "The fitter said he hadn't seen him either."

A tiny alarm bell went off in the back of my mind.

"It's not like him not to come back for food," I said. "He probably heard all the banging and decided to stay away."

"I hope he's okay," Stephanie frowned. She was worried too.

I didn't want to give a voice to the worry that was nibbling away at me: that Alvin had come in, seen the open front door and darted out into the main road. The consequences were unthinkable.

"He'll come back later when he realises the workers have gone," I reassured her, but we were both thinking the same thing.

"He wouldn't have gone out the front," we both agreed.

Alvin didn't return that evening. At intervals we went out in the garden and called him, then went walking down the alley and into the lane, shaking his dry food. One of the neighbours was outside her flat and we asked if she'd seen him. She hadn't. Stephanie sent texts to the other neighbours to ask if they'd seen him too. No one had.

That night I went to bed expecting him to be on his bed in the conservatory the following morning but when I got up and went downstairs to look through the glass panel in the kitchen door, he wasn't there. Sometimes he waited outdoors under the trees until he saw a light come on and then darted through the cat flap like a rocket. Or I'd hear him scrambling over the fence from the neighbour's garden. But there was silence, which only amplified the little voice in my head telling me something was amiss.

Later that morning we went out again and walked further afield, calling his name, shaking his food, checking down *cul de sacs*, alleyways and behind sheds. Throughout the day I expected him to turn up and comforted myself with the knowledge that he had been away before and his absence wasn't completely out of character. I used the same argument the following morning when, once again, he wasn't there. But by that time the argument was running thin. It was summer when he'd previously gone AWOL and although he was a night owl and enjoyed prowling in the dark, he wasn't a lover of the cold, damp weather, so it was out of character for him to choose to stay away from the warmth and shelter of the house.

By the second morning we both knew something was very wrong.

"I'm sure he hasn't got out on the road, but perhaps we should check," Stephanie suggested. That morning we put work on hold and scoured along the main road and the side streets leading off it, looking under hedges and in front gardens. Neither said it, but we were looking for a body. It was horrible. I was haunted by the thought that he had been hit by a car, and lay injured, terrified, cold and in pain under a hedge or bush, crying out to be saved. The image kept running through my mind and I tried to rationalise my fear. It was highly unlikely that he would have run straight through the house and out the front door. Whenever he came into the house he would always come and find one of us to say hello and to see if there was a chance of a treat. But the longer the day went on without any sign of him, the harder it became to convince myself that nothing bad had happened.

Our search was fruitless. We knocked on every neighbour's door and asked people to check in sheds and garages. That evening we made a missing poster of him and printed several copies. The following morning there was still no sign of him, so we went out and placed the posters in prominent places where there was maximum footfall. We stuck them to lampposts, in the local shop windows and further afield on the noticeboards at the library and the railway station. Later in the day I walked past the Co-op on the corner of the lane and Alvin's little face stared out at me from a poster the staff had kindly put in the door. I vowed to find him no matter what, and went home to start researching.

Stephanie and I worked together as a team. Neither of us voiced our fears to the other and we tried to keep each other positive.

Anyone who has ever lost a pet will understand the sense of helplessness and worry that takes hold. The not-knowing was awful – all I had were hypothetical scenarios. Alvin had gone of his own volition (which I thought unlikely as he seemed to like living where he did, and all his needs were met), he'd been taken by someone (more likely, I suspected, as he was a friendly, handsome cat), he was locked in somewhere, or he'd come to grief in an accident and was either dead or injured.

With trepidation I called the local authority. Under UK law, any motorist who hits a dog, horse, cow, pig, goat, sheep, donkey or mule is required to stop and notify the police. Cats do not fall under the regulation and anyone who finds a dead one on the road is advised to contact the local authority. Not all councils scan the bodies of road-kill cats but our one, Mole Valley District Council, did, and endeavoured to contact owners should the worst happen. I spoke to one of the Environmental Officers who had the grim task of keeping the borough's dead cat ledger and was relieved to learn that Alvin was not included in the week's roll call of fallen moggies. Next, Stephanie called the vet where he was registered, as their information was contained on his microchip, so, if he had been found and handed to another vet to have his details scanned, they would have been contacted. The receptionist had no record.

Over the following hours Operation Alvin swung into action. We placed missing notices on a range of websites including Gumtree and local Facebook groups. We contacted Animal Search UK, which runs a large internet database of lost and found pets and offered several levels of service. These included the production of waterproof posters and access to a confidential 24-hour manned phone line that took tip-offs from anyone who had information and notified owners immediately of any sightings. The confidentiality was designed to encourage people who may not wish to contact owners directly, perhaps fearing they were in trouble for feeding a cat that wasn't their own. The luxury level service included the immediate deployment of a specialist search party who, for £1,600, would scour the area and conduct a systematic door-to-door search. We choose a £260 option that included posters and the phone line. We were advised to offer an undisclosed reward and ordered the posters to be couriered the next day.

They read: "Reward. Missing. Alvin was last seen on Wednesday 3 February 2016 in Surrey KT21. He has been castrated and CANNOT be used for breeding." I winced at the thought that such personal details would be plastered over every lamp-post in the vicinity.

The posters arrived the next day and Alvin was assigned his own reference number. He was 244769. "Already a statistic," I thought to myself mournfully. We ordered 200 and spent half a day posting them through every letterbox within a half-mile radius. When the kids came, they were sent out on leaflet duty too. They were as concerned as we were about his disappearance but I remained positive and explained that he'd probably just wandered off somewhere and got lost.

The days passed and calls started to filter through. There were sightings of strays from miles away. Some people called in sightings more out of optimism than anything else. It was highly unlikely he'd managed to travel across Greater London to Greenwich, which was where one sighting came from. Other people were clearly deluded. One lady, Pauline, phoned two days running to report sightings 12 miles apart.

"He chased me," she explained, breathless as if it had just happened. "I was scared."

She was convinced it was him. I was convinced she was suffering from mental health problems and suspicious she was motivated by the advertised reward.

"It looked just like him," she offered when I explained, during her second call, that he didn't have a car or driving licence so was unlikely to have covered so much ground in a day.

To Stephanie, who was increasingly upset by his disappearance, I continued to put on a positive front.

"He'll be in a house nearby, being fed kippers by a well-meaning elderly spinster," I told her. Secretly though, in darker moments, I feared the worst.

"What if something's happened to him?" she asked.

"He's very independent. He'll be able to survive fine if he's lost somewhere. And he's sociable, he'll persuade someone to feed him," I reasoned.

The sightings we heard of in and around Ashtead were of more interest. On several occasions someone from the helpline called with information of a sighting and one of us would get in the car and drive to the locations given, where we searched in vain. People left their contact details and I called them back for more details. It was always too late. The cats they had seen had always gone by the time one of us arrived. People took photos of strays and sent them in. A week went by. There was still no firm news, but two patterns started to emerge. Several sightings were reported in a cluster of roads on the other side of the main road. If it was Alvin, he had indeed bolted through the front door and managed to survive the crossing and was then lost on the other side. In the other direction, several people called to say they had seen a cat matching his description in and around a nearby *cul de sac*.

Every hour around 60 pets go missing in the UK, according to Sainsbury's Pet Insurance. Their sad little faces peer out from posters taped to lamp-posts while social media echoes with the desperate pleas of their owners. Alvin became one of the vanished; his memory was kept alive by the posters we strung up on the A24 between Epsom and Leatherhead and in the repeated messages we posted on the local community Facebook page.

As the days turned into a week I started to look at other search options and spoke to a drone company that specialised in tracking down missing pets.

"We get an aerial view of the terrain, so it works particularly well if you live in an area that is quite built up and has a lot of hard-to-access places," I was told.

I spoke to a man who owned a tracker dog that could potentially sniff out lost cats. He explained that the fresher the trail, the better the chance of success. But by that time Alvin had been gone for over a week so the chances of him being tracked down by a sniffer dog were slim.

I also spoke to one of the UK's most successful missing pet investigation agencies, The Pet Detectives. The Surrey-based company was run by private investigator and former CID detective Colin Butcher.

"Usually in the first few minutes we can work out whether we are dealing with a lost cat or a stolen cat and sometimes we are called to deal with ownership disputes," he told me. "There are certain breeds of cats such as Russian Blues and British Short-haired that are personable and pretty, which make them more attractive for thieves."

According to the pet PI, cats with friendly temperaments were more likely to befriend neighbours who could then get attached to them.

"In some cases, people will even give the cat another name, tempt them into the house and then it's only a matter of time before they assume ownership," he said. "It's wilful blindness. I've met so many people who have taken cats, they come from all walks of life, they are families, single people, and they always use the excuse it was a stray. If a healthy cat comes into your garden wearing a collar, it might be disorientated but it is certainly not a stray. In most cases the cat is just being curious because it picked up a smell."

He told me about a recent case where a young male cat had gone missing after being "beaten up" by an older tom in the neighbourhood.

"It happens a lot when a female in the neighbourhood comes into season," he explained. The female had upset the balance of the feline community and the cat in question had moved on and found a new home in less crowded territory. This cat migration, I discovered, was common. Colin had carried out a research project for the BBC Horizon documentary *The Secret Life of Cats* in which he and his team monitored the movements of a whole village's cat population. They discovered that two out of three of the cats went into other people's houses on a day-to-day basis.

"That's what gets them into trouble," he told me. "People adopt them, and they might lock the cat flap for a couple of weeks to try and get the cat to stay put, which puts the owner through hell. It pulls their world apart."

The realisation dawned on me. Perhaps that was what happened to Alvin. All the pieces of the puzzle seemed to fit. A small female cat had arrived in the neighbourhood a few weeks before he disappeared. Perhaps her appearance had upset the balance in the feline community and Alvin, being the smallest and a relative newcomer, had wandered off and into someone else's home, where he'd been catnapped.

"Cat thieves are opportunists, they are normally your neighbours," Colin warned. "They differ from dog thieves who are usually specialists making a living stealing specific dogs which are then supplied to small breeders. They target the most commercial breeds, such as springer spaniels, which have large litters. There is an enormous, unregulated black market in stolen dogs."

Some people, I learned, become obsessive about taking in cats and hoard them. They convince themselves the cats they take in are stray or neglected and that they are doing the right thing by abducting them. Colin called it Noah's Ark syndrome.

"They genuinely believe they are the only opportunity that cat has of surviving and that they give the animal a better home, even if they live in wretched conditions. They still think they are doing a better job than the owner."

The Pet Detectives success rate was impressive. They recovered 80 percent of the cases they took on and when I spoke to them, they had already taken five cat cases that year and recovered every one. But as we chatted it became apparent that Alvin's case was not one they could help with as by that time he had been gone for almost two weeks. Colin explained that time was of the essence and if a cat had been missing in a built-up area for a couple of weeks, there was little they could do. In each of the cases he mentioned, the owners had employed the detectives within a week of the cat going missing.

"If we get in early we are usually able to establish why it went missing and where it's going to be and who has it. Every cat we have taken on this year has been a young male tom between 10 months and two years, because at this time of year we get a lot of displacement where the older toms become territorial and push the younger ones out."

Colin's words again reinforced the theory that Alvin had been pushed out of the community. My heart broke thinking about it. I imagined him slinking off into the sunset, like Dick Whittington, scared and lonely because he no longer felt he was welcome in his own home. All I could hope was that if he had found a new home, he was being looked after and had somewhere warm and safe to stay. He was more than capable of looking after himself and catching his own food, but he did like to sit in front of the fire and enjoyed the comfort of a warm bed and scratch behind the ear. Colin confirmed what I had begun to realise. Cats are incredibly fickle. They can up and leave for the smallest of reasons and they make the decision to go consciously, whereas when a dog goes missing, it's usually because it has got itself lost accidentally.

"You only have to move an armchair and a cat will leave," he said. I thought about the changes to the garden. To us humans they were home improvements, to Alvin they would have been earthquakes. Cats map out their environments by scent. If you change or move something, the cat's scent map becomes disrupted. Alvin wouldn't have known whether he was coming or going. I had the sickening feeling that in part, we were responsible for his departure, which made us equally responsible for any misfortune that had befallen him.

Colin's words rang true on many levels. The circumstantial evidence suggested that Alvin had gone AWOL because there was a new lady cat in town and that he'd happened upon a neighbour who, misguidedly, had started to feed him and had eventually enticed him to stay, or locked him in.

This theory was given extra credence from an anonymous tip-off we received several days later. A lady called to say that a cat matching Alvin's description had been seen hanging around a large property in a nearby close, belonging to an elderly neighbour who was notorious for feeding other people's cats. The property was located in an area from where we had already received a cluster of sightings. I started my own detective work and spoke to several people who knew the woman in question and they all confirmed that she had form as exactly the sort of catnapping, Noah's Ark syndrome-suffering individual Colin had spoken about. She habitually lured cats to her garden with food and treats and let them stay in her home on a relaxed come-and-go basis, and even when neighbours explained that perhaps the cats had owners and should not be encouraged, she maintained that she was doing nothing wrong.

I found myself in a very delicate situation. The lady was elderly and clearly a little confused. I didn't know what she was capable of and did not want to upset her or give her a reason to lock Alvin away somewhere, if indeed he was there.

We formulated a plan. First, I did another leaflet drop in the road where she lived, making sure I put a leaflet through her door. Then, later in the day, Stephanie knocked to explain that she was Alvin's owner, had received a sighting in the area and was going house to house to see if anyone knew where he was. She was careful not to apportion any blame or alert the lady to the fact that she had been specifically identified as a potential catnapper.

The lady looked at the poster Stephanie held and nodded slowly.

"I might have seen him, cats seem to like it round here. I've got a large garden so they come here quite a lot," she said.

She was in her eighties and despite a slight stoop, seemed in good health and in command of all her faculties.

Then Stephanie told a little white lie that we hoped would appeal to the lady's better nature.

"You see, he has to take regular medication and without it he could die, so it's really important that we find him," she said earnestly. "Can I leave my number with you and the number of my partner and if you see him or any cat that looks like him, please can you call. You could save his life."

The ploy seemed to do the trick and the woman took our numbers and agreed. Stephanie also took her number and asked if it was okay to check in now and then, just in case the woman forgot.

Sure as cats are cats, later in the evening the woman called me.

"I think he's been here," she said. "He's not here now, but I'm sure it was him." I bit my knuckle in frustration.

"That's wonderful," I mock-soothed, "do you think if he comes again, maybe you could call when he's there?"

"Yes of course," she said. And then as an afterthought. "He looked very well and happy, as if he is being fed and looked after."

"I bet he is," I thought.

We heard nothing for several days but went to the area outside her house regularly to call him and to search. We must have looked such a sad sight, regularly walking the street, forlornly calling his name, shaking packets of Dreamies and a small white toy mouse with a rattle in it that he used to play with. There was no sign.

Then, three days later, she called again.

"I've just seen him," she said.

I ran to her house, two minutes away, and knocked on the wooden door.

"He was in the bushes," she said, ushering me through. It was a large, well-kept detached house on a corner plot with a big, mature garden. As she walked me through the house we went through the kitchen and a conservatory that ran the width of the back of the property. In both there were litter trays, cat toys and food and water bowls.

"How many cats have you got?" I asked casually.

"None," she replied nonchalantly, "I sometimes look after some for my friends."

Something smelt very fishy, and it wasn't just the Sheba.

Outside, I wandered around her garden, calling again, listening for sounds of cat activity in the bushes. I stayed for 20 minutes, my calls becoming increasingly frustrated. In the end I sighed and left, asking her to call again if the cat returned. She explained that the moggy that might be Alvin usually turned up in the evening, so later I called her. She told me he wasn't there. I went and stood on the pavement outside her house anyway and called his name. Again, there was nothing and I left, worried that I was turning into some sort of obsessive.

Several days passed and there were no sightings. The cat lady didn't call back. Some more random calls filtered through, none of which were feasible and several of which were, once again, phoned through by people who seemed to have a loose grasp on reality. One woman even called to say she was psychic and had a premonition that Alvin had been taken away by a man in a brown Ford. The one comfort we had was that the longer it went on, the less likely it was that he'd had an accident, as a vet would have notified us if he had been taken in and so would the local authority if his body had been found. Instead we were left in limbo. All we could do was wait and hope. Life went on, but regularly I'd find myself thinking about him, worrying where he was and, in those moments, a melancholy feeling of loss nagged at me.

Stephanie and I worked well together throughout "Operation Alvin". Despite the worry we both kept cool heads and reassured each other that he would come back. As the weeks went by, we both realised that the chance he would return home of his own volition was becoming increasingly unlikely but we bolstered each other with tales of other missing cats who had returned months after vanishing. Several people we spoke to in that time had their own anecdotes. One couple we knew had a cat that came home a full nine months after going AWOL. It just reappeared at their back door one day.

I felt powerless and empty, but not panicked or grief-stricken. There was no evidence to suggest that anything bad had happened to him. On the contrary, the evidence suggested he chose to go. In a way, ironically, I had been hoodwinked and then abandoned. Alvin had done the mother of all honeytraps on me. I spurned him initially, he'd manipulated me to a point where I was attached to him, and then he'd gone. I tried to be circumspect and stoic. I reasoned that like all cat owners, I had entered into a pact when I got my pet. I knew that cats were independent and only loyal to a point. Ultimately, they were selfish and did what suited them. They were wont to wander if they so desired and that's what happened, it was part of the deal.

Then, several weeks after he'd gone, we got what I hoped was our break. A man, who sounded completely normal and sane, called to report a sighting in his garden less than a mile away. I checked on a map and tried to think like a cat. Assuming Alvin had been hanging out for a few days at the suspected catnapper's house, the route from there to the scene of the new sighting made perfect cat sense. It would have taken him across the grounds of a private school and through woodland where there were ponds with ducks and other small mammals. The gentleman explained that he'd not seen the cat before and wasn't in the habit of calling in cat sightings, but he'd seen one of our posters and was convinced that the cat which had recently started to visit his garden was Alvin.

"We have a cat as well and leave her food by the back door, he comes to eat it. He's friendly enough and his markings are the same as the one on the poster. I'd say I was 90 percent sure it's your cat," he said.

It was remarkable news. Over three weeks had gone by and I was beginning to lose hope. Colin had said that the trail goes cold after several weeks so if it was Alvin, we were lucky.

"You're welcome to come round and see if he'll come if you call him," the man offered. So we grabbed the carrier, some treats and the toy mouse and sped to the address, which was just near Epsom Downs in a small village called Langley Vale. The house was a large detached farm cottage set in well over an acre of gardens. There was a line of tall fir trees along one border and a wooded corner shielding an outhouse and garage to the side. The whole site was open and beyond the trees there was open land and a horse stables. The man came out and led us around the back of the property to where the cat had been seen.

Once again he said he was certain the cat he had seen was the cat in the poster. He offered us a cup of tea and explained that we could take as long as we needed. We set about pacing through his grounds, calling and shaking the mouse. Once again I felt slightly self-conscious. After about 15 minutes the man came out with two cups of tea and we sat on a bench with him and had a chat.

"I really hope it is your cat," he said. "It would be lovely to have a happy ending."

After another 20 minutes the cold and dark set in and we decided to give up the search party. We said our goodbyes and the man said he'd call as soon as he saw the cat again. Sure enough, two days later when Stephanie was in the hairdresser, he phoned.

"He's here," he said. "I've put some food out to try and keep him here. Don't worry about knocking, just go straight round the back."

I grabbed the carrier and some treats, ran to the car and drove to the house, where I jumped out and ran round the back, forgetting to get the carrier from the back of the car. It was dark and in the gloom, silhouetted against the light coming through the back door, stood a cat. It cast a long shadow across the lawn.

"Hey Alvin," I said gently.

He turned his head.

I still couldn't see him clearly because of the dark but he was the same proportions and generally had the same markings. He even had big ears.

"Alvin, it's me."

He looked over at me with wide, quizzical eyes. He seemed nervous, so I stayed back and crouched down.

"Hey boy, its me."

My heart was thumping. Slowly the cat walked towards me. I reasoned with myself. He'd been stray for several weeks. Who knows what could have happened in that time; he was probably semi-feral and would need time to adjust. Of course he'd be wary.

"It's okay Alvin, we can go home now," I said gently.

I could see the man looking out the kitchen window at us, smiling.

As the cat got closer I could see him more clearly.

"It's you isn't it, Alvin?" I said. There was a lump in my throat. I blinked back tears.

"Where have you been, you silly thing?" I smiled. The cat came close enough to sniff my hand. I noticed he looked darker. "He's just dirty," I thought to myself, "he'll need a bath."

I reached out to stroke him, and he backed off, turned and walked away. Surely he hadn't forgotten me already, or perhaps he'd had some kind of accident and sustained amnesia. I got up and followed him. He wasn't bothered by me and walked slowly. He stopped again and let me stroke him. His coat felt coarse and oily. He was definitely dirty.

"Shall we go home Alvin?" I said gently. I reached out and he let me stroke him. He started purring.

"Oh Alvin," I said, my eyes moist. I surprised myself. I was crying with relief. I gently put my hands around him and lifted him up. We were going home.

I walked him round the side of the house. He looked perplexed, but let me take him. The man came out.

"It's him," I said, sniffing back tears, "it's Alvin."

Then I remembered the carrier.

"Shit, can you get the carrier out the back of my car please?" I asked.

The man ran round to the vehicle and tried the handle. It was locked.

"Where are the keys," he called.

"In my pocket," I said.

I quickened my pace because I felt Alvin becoming tense.

"It's okay, I've got one you can borrow," the man said.

"Can you hurry please," I called, "I think he's spooked."

I tightened my grip and he started to struggle. I felt him tense up as a claw sunk deep into my shoulder. I tried to soothe him with a calm voice as he began to wriggle. I held him fast against my chest. He started to rake his claws around my neck and made a low groan.

Thankfully the man appeared with an old wooden animal carrier. He could see the urgency in my eyes and put it on the floor in front of me. By now, one paw was attached to my shoulder by several claws which had sunk into my skin. I pulled the cat away from me to unhook the talons and unceremoniously stuffed him in the box and shut the door.

I explained to the man that Alvin was most likely disorientated and confused and that he'd need to go home and have a quiet period to calm down. Inside the wooden box, the cat was meowing.

I stood there for a minute looking at it and once again felt emotional. The man saw me blinking and stepped over to me. He put his hand on my shoulder.

"It's okay to cry," he said. "They're one of the family aren't they? It's a happy ending. You go home and get him settled. There's no rush to bring the carrier back."

I nodded, took a breath, composed myself, picked up the box and put it in the back of the car. On the short drive home I spoke to Alvin to calm him. He never did like car journeys very much.

"Where have you been fella?" I asked. He meowed. "I bet you could tell some stories." He smelled musty. "You're going to need a bath," I told him. I knew Stephanie was still out and was excited about the prospect of surprising her when she came in. I decided not to text and tell her. Halfway home Alvin went quiet for a minute and I stopped talking. A new scent permeated the car.

"Christ Alvin!" I gagged. "Couldn't you have waited?"

He'd crapped in the crate, and it reeked. I opened the windows.

When we arrived at home I carefully lifted the box out of the car, so as not to spill any leakage, and gingerly carried it to the conservatory. I didn't want to release Alvin into the back garden in case he ran off again. I knew he'd need several days of adjustment indoors to acclimatise and so I shut the door to the garden, opened the kitchen door and opened the wire trap on the carrier. I stood back to allow him to come out in his own time.

"You're home," I told him.

He poked a curious head out of the carrier and carefully crept out. He looked around inquisitively and sniffed the air, although I doubted he could smell anything apart from the rancid stench of his own faeces. I was glad to see him, but my stomach was churning.

He slowly walked into the kitchen and I quickly shut the door behind him and threw the carrier into the garden. I then followed him into the house.

In the light he looked like Alvin, but slightly different. He was thinner and darker, and the musty smell clung to him. Of course, he would be thinner, I told myself, he hasn't been eating properly, and he was darker because he was dirty. He allowed me to stroke him and I gave him some food, which he ate gratefully. I stood and looked at him, really scrutinising him. He was Alvin, I was sure of it (I had invested so much hope that this was the big break that perhaps I was trying to convince myself. This cat was like Tinkerbell. If I believed enough, it would be real). His behaviour was subdued and he seemed wary of the surroundings but I was sure this was just a consequence of his experiences. Who knew what he'd been through? I pushed the nagging doubt to one side and went to get his bed, which we had kept in its usual place on top of the tumble dryer in the conservatory. When I came back in the room he was on the dining room table, sniffing around.

BE

NICE

OR

LEAVE

Alvin helps Nick
with his work.

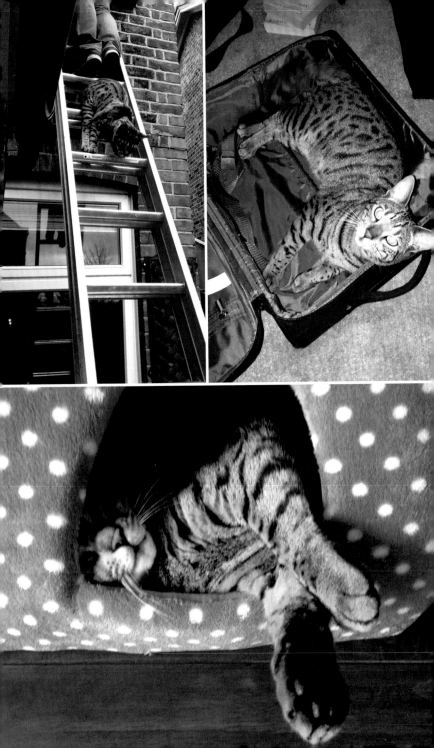

Clockwise from top: Stephanie has totally convinced Nick that Alvin is a great idea; leaving his mark on Nick; climbing up his chimney; sleeping with his legs hanging out; mastering ladders; making his feelings about an impending trip felt...

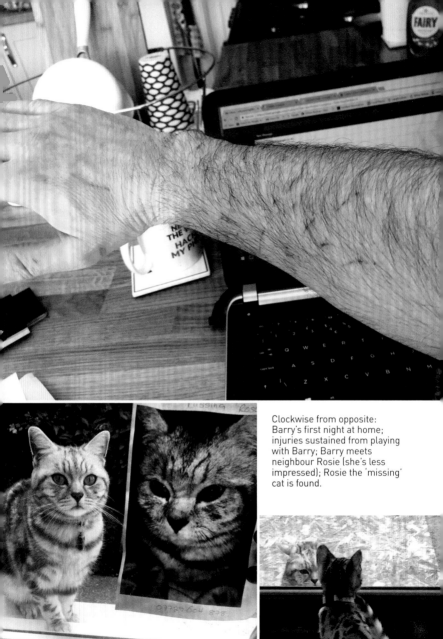

Clockwise from opposite: Barry's first night at home; injuries sustained from playing with Barry; Barry meets neighbour Rosie (she's less impressed); Rosie the 'missing' cat is found.

Clockwise from left:
Barry in the sink;
Nick with Barry;
Barry being 'groomed';
Barry rejects a toy
in favour of the box;
Barry's first 'kill'.

Barry in all
his cat majesty.

I put the bed on the floor and heard the back door open.

"Jesus, what's that smell," Stephanie called.

I couldn't contain myself.

"I've got a surprise for you," I called back.

Stephanie ran into the room.

"He's back!" she squealed.

Then she took a look at the cat standing on the table, stopped in her tracks and frowned.

"That's not Alvin!" she said.

"It is," I argued, "look at his markings, he's just dirty."

She squinted.

"Alvin?" she asked.

He looked at her.

"Honestly, it's him," I affirmed.

"Did he recognise you when you went to get him?" she asked.

"Sort of," I replied. "He was a bit apprehensive, but he's been away for weeks, of course he's going to be wary."

"It looks like him," she admitted, "but I don't think it is."

We then called up photos of Alvin on our phones and scrutinised the markings, which were seemingly identical, but the photos we had were all taken from different angles, so we couldn't be 100 percent sure.

Meanwhile, the cat walked over to the bed and sniffed it. Then it climbed in.

"You see, it is him," I said excitedly.

It then sprayed on it.

"Alvin never did that!" I frowned.

Stephanie then asked a very important question. Had I checked whether the cat that I'd brought back was neutered? No, I hadn't.

"Hmm," said Stephanie.

I was beginning to feel prickly with embarrassment and disappointment and picked the cat up and put him on the table again, turning him to face away from us. There, just under his tail, was a soft cushion of downy fur.

"He's got nuts," said Stephanie.

But here's the thing. After Alvin was neutered, his scrotum never flattened, so from appearances he looked like he was still intact. I reminded Stephanie of this.

"Someone will have to check."

Stephanie sighed.

Throughout our relationship, I had a habit of getting myself into mishaps and awkward situations.

"This could only happen to you, couldn't it?" she said, and told me to hold the cat. I did while she carefully poked around in the doppelganger's private area. He let out an indignant grunt. Anyone who walked into the dining room at that point would have called the RSPCA, or Childline.

"He's definitely got balls," confirmed Stephanie.

"What have I done?" I said.

"You've abducted a cat and we've just molested it," she answered, deadpan.

The cat slunk quietly off the table and padded across the floor back to the food bowl where it comforted itself with some more Purina salmon kibble.

"Comfort-eating to dull the shame," I commented.

I then had to make one of the most embarrassing telephone calls of my life. We couldn't keep the cat and for all we knew, it might belong to someone. There were stables backing on to the property where I took it from, and it was likely the resident mouser. So I called the man from whose garden I'd liberated it, and who had, half an hour previously, celebrated the emotional reunion with me.

"You know that cat I took? Turns out it's not Alvin after all. Alvin had been done, this one hasn't. Do you mind if I come back and release it?"

He was perplexed but agreed.

"Oh, and it crapped in your carrier. I'll give it a hose down, but you might want to leave it out to air," I said.

After a clean-up, I gently coaxed the cat back into the carrier. He didn't struggle – he was probably traumatised and glad to be somewhere secure. I drove quietly back to the house, parked in the driveway and carried the cat round to the back garden where I opened the door. Alvin's smelly double walked out, took a few steps forward and looked back at me.

"Sorry," I mouthed. And with that he trotted off into the dark.

I didn't knock. I placed the carrier by the front door along with a bottle of wine I'd bought as a thank you and an apology and got back in the car.

There were no more sightings of Alvin or any cats matching his description after that. Alvin had gone and his absence left a huge cat-shaped hole in my life.

CHAPTER EIGHT

CATASTROPHE

We often found ourselves wondering where he was and what he was doing. We'd make up scenarios.

"He's probably found a big house with an open fire and ingratiated himself with the owners by catching a load of mice," I mused.

"Maybe he climbed into someone's car and is now living on the coast, near a fishing harbour," imagined Stephanie.

To the children I was optimistic.

"He'll turn up at some point," I reassured. "It's what cats do. He'll be somewhere and he'll be perfectly happy and then one day, for some reason a vet will scan his chip and someone will call up and say: 'We have your cat'."

To a degree they trusted my optimism but I think deep down they too realised that the chances of his return were slim.

There's never a good time to be the owner of a missing cat. Worry, uncertainty, delayed grief, frustration, heartache, powerlessness: these, I realised, were the feelings of the owners left behind when their cats disappeared. Whereas before I became a pet owner I would have glibly discounted the emotional cost of a missing pet, I now understood why people will go to such lengths to recover their lost companions. I had battled against having a cat and having got one I struggled with the growing acceptance that Alvin was part of the family. The reality was that he wasn't. If he was a child, there would have been police search parties, media appeals, private detectives and no expense spared to recover him. We did much to try and find him, but we didn't do enough, because he remained missing and I felt guilty when, after several weeks, our efforts were scaled back and life went on as normal. I reasoned with myself: "What else can you do? Life has to go on." Yet others had offered huge rewards and kept searching for their missing moggies for months. In the US the owners of four felines thought to have perished in a fire offered a combined $100,000 for their return after sightings were confirmed in nearby woodland. Two of the missing moggies were Guinness World Record holders: one had the longest tail in the world, while the other stood 20.1 inches tall, which was also a record.

Our trail had gone cold and we were left in limbo. There were thousands and thousands of people just like me, wondering what happened to their pets, hopeful that they were safe and well, encouraged by every story of someone else's cat that returned home after long periods away. There are stories of cats missing for years and returning home. A cat named Winston from Cornwall went AWOL for 15 years before his original owners got a call from a vet 35 miles away to inform them that he had been found wandering down a country road looking frail. He had disappeared after the family moved house and no one knew what had happened to him in the intervening years. Winston was only one when he went missing. By the time he got back home he was an OAP.

My loss was amplified by another fear that I never mentioned to anyone because I didn't even want to countenance the possibility that it might have happened. At the time Alvin went missing, news stories had begun to circulate of a horrific crime spree that was happening a few miles away. There was a serial killer on the loose and he was targeting cats. Initially, he was dubbed the Croydon Cat Killer but renamed the M25 Animal Killer in subsequent years as his blood lust, species choice and geographical range increased. His particular circle of hell encompassed London and the home counties and included foxes, rabbits and a baby owl. There were confirmed killings in the Isle of Wight, Kent, Birmingham, Wirral and Sheffield, leading investigators to conclude that his job involved travel. In the three years after his first confirmed victim in 2015, he was believed to have carried out over 370 killings, and when Alvin went missing, one of his victims was just a few miles away (a year later there was also one in Ashtead).

The first recorded victim was Ukiyo, a ragdoll cross. It was taken five months before Alvin disappeared from Addiscombe near Croydon in September 2015 and discovered by its horrified owner when it had been mutilated and placed prominently so it would be found. Within months, the killer had struck several more times and extended his range to the town of Sutton, just a few miles away from our home. In all confirmed cases the *modus operandi* was the same. The killer bludgeoned the cat to death with a blunt instrument, then waited at least half an hour for the blood to coagulate before mutilating the body. He precisely severed heads and tails with a sharp knife. If he had time, he removed organs and pelvis. The killer sometimes took carcasses away with him, returning days later to crime scenes to place them in easy view. The mutilated corpses were then left on display in a specific signature position for owners and anyone else to find. Cats were left on front lawns, doorsteps and on top of cars.

The numbers soon rose. Within a few months of Ukiyo's death he was believed to have killed over 50 animals and the escalation prompted actor and cat-lover Martin Clunes to write to the Met Police commissioner at the time on behalf of the animal rights group Peta.

The *Doc Martin* actor wrote: "I read with horror that some of the cats had been decapitated and dismembered – this is the stuff of nightmares. The local community is understandably distraught and frightened. No one feels safe while this sick individual is on the loose."

He added: "Research in psychology and criminology shows that people who commit acts of cruelty to animals don't stop there – many of them move on to their fellow humans. That is a scary thought indeed."

He implored the police to take every measure necessary to catch the criminal, warning that "the safety of the entire community depends on it."

Peta offered a £5,000 reward, as did charity Outpaced. James McVey, lead guitarist of the Vamps and cat lover, offered gig tickets and called the killer "scum".

The killer cast a dark shadow over every cat owner in London, the home counties and beyond. And with an estimated 700 cats per square mile, he had a lot of victims to choose from. It was easy pickings. He lured his prey with pet food, crab sticks or raw chicken.

Initially police said it was the work of foxes or road traffic accidents. But a Croydon-based animal welfare group, South Norwood Animal Rescue and Liberty, or Snarl, started seeing Facebook posts about the killings and realised there was a pattern. The group was run by partners Tony Jenkins and Boudicca Rising. South African Boudicca was a self-described mad cat lady who had been involved in animal rescue since arriving in Britain in 1994. When she and fellow animal-lover, Tony, became a couple, they set up their own animal protection charity. When they first realised there was a cat-killing spree on their doorstep, they thought it could be the work of a gang. In the face of police reluctance, they started a media campaign to rattle the rusty cages of officialdom and after a rash of attention-grabbing headlines, the cops started to take notice. Snarl provided details of killings and spoke out at a 2015 Croydon community meeting attended by the then head of the Metropolitan Police, Sir Bernard Hogan Howe.

In response, in December 2015, the Met set up a joint investigation with the RSPCA and Snarl, code-named Operation Takahe (a randomly assigned moniker that is the name of a flightless bird from New Zealand). The 12-strong team was headed by Detective Sergeant Andy Collin, who feared it was only a matter of time before the killer turned his attention to humans, as serial killers often begin their careers by harming animals.

Snarl became the first port of call for new victims and operated a triage service for the police, urging anyone who found a body to call them first so they could establish which deaths were caused by the killer, and which were caused by road accidents or other acts of cruelty. When a victim was found, they helped secure the crime scene, checked the animal's microchip and scoured the ground for clues. But leads and clues were difficult to find. The killer was methodical and clinical. Surrey University's forensic animal lab reviewed some of the cases but it is almost impossible to gather DNA from cat fur, and even if some were collected, there could be no guarantees it would be from the killer.

Anyone with a missing cat, particularly in and around London and the Home Counties, faced the added agony of worrying whether their pet had become one of the hundreds of victims. The more I read, however, the more I could discount this horrific scenario. The M25 Animal Killer received his gratification from the imagined reaction of the pet owners and the people who found his horrifying exhibits. He didn't hide the bodies of his victims and if Alvin had been one of them, we would have discovered him.

Alvin remained lost and in my own way I grieved for him. I missed him and thought about him and wondered if, in his tiny cat brain, he was missing me too. Whenever I imagined him I felt a wave of melancholy. I wasn't mourning, it was more of a nagging sadness. It was loss. I missed him being around. I missed seeing his legs poking out from the side of his bed in the morning. Thanks to David Attenborough, I knew he couldn't love me, but he had certainly shown affection and there was plenty of evidence to demonstrate that animals can at least display a rudimentary sense of loss. Creatures as diverse as dolphins, dogs and apes have all been seen to appear grief-stricken. Elephants have been observed holding vigils over the bodies of members of their herd. A two-year-old African elephant at a zoo in Hungary stayed with its mother for 14 hours after she died and continued to cry and show signs of distress after the body was removed. Similar behaviour was seen in 2008 when a gorilla at a German zoo mourned the death of her three-month-old baby. She carried his body around for almost a week and refused to let anyone take it away.

In darker moments, I pondered the metaphysical realm. If Alvin had passed over, would I ever know? Could he contact me through a ghostly apparition? Did he have a soul? Several years before I owned a cat, I had spent time with one of the UK's most popular mediums, Sally Morgan. We'd discussed spirituality and animal psychic ability at length and if she was right, I needed to look for signs from Alvin as dead or alive. He had the ability to reach through the netherworld and let me know he was okay, either on Earth-plane or in spirit.

"Animals not only have souls, they are also psychic," Sally had explained. "Their energy is pure because they haven't been tainted and they are much more in tune with instinct and intuition than humans are. Anyone who owns a cat or a dog will know what I'm talking about."

She had three psychic bulldogs and explained that they saw spirits all the time.

"They can be lying there, snoozing away when suddenly they'll sit bolt upright, look intently at what appears to be empty space and then run off chasing something that isn't there to the untrained eye," she said.

Alvin used to do something similar, but usually he was just chasing a fly, or a shadow.

Sally had been seeing human and animal spirits all her life including dogs, cats and even a seal. One of her dogs, Holly, was tragically run over and died. Sally admitted she went to pieces for a week after the accident and was so grief-stricken she stayed in bed and couldn't work. In the depths of her despair Holly appeared to her, to offer comfort.

"It was early in the morning. I'd cried myself to sleep the night before and dreamt vividly about her all that night," said Sally. "The dreams were her signs to me. I was just waking up and as I opened my eyes I saw her face looking down at me. She was sitting on my chest staring at me. I blinked, confused at first. For a split second I thought maybe her death had been a terrible dream. I cried her name and went to stroke her but my hand went straight through the apparition. It was beautiful to know that her spirit was there with me but still so sad because she was dead. I cried as the image faded and I still well up with emotion when I remember it."

I wondered if Alvin would come to me and sit on my chest. One of the small advantages of him not being around was that I was sleeping much better, so I had mixed feelings about the ghost dream scenario.

Sally believed that psychic ability was the natural capability to plug into the energy that exists around all life. She said it was about following intuition, and that humans lost the ability to trust their instincts and read the signs long ago, but that animals were still very much plugged into the realm of supernatural energy. Some of what she said struck a chord. Alvin always knew when we were going away days before we left, and would sulk and become clingy. He knew that when the suitcase came out one of us would be going somewhere, and usually climbed inside it.

"They understand more than we realise," said Sally.

I felt silly dwelling on these thoughts. I had been cynical and nonchalant about cat ownership at the beginning, yet there I was, twisting myself up about Alvin's afterlife, or lack thereof. In the spring Stephanie and I went on a weekend break to Paris. She had some work there and we tacked a few extra nights on. In Sacre Coeur I lit a candle for Alvin. I'm not religious at all, but it just seemed like a fitting thing to do. It was a gesture to mark the fact that I missed him. In Montmartre I bought a Le Chat Noir fridge magnet.

Later, I even started to investigate the possibility of cat cloning, not because I thought that was an option, but because since losing a pet, I had been become interested in the types of options open to grieving owners. In the US, there was a company called ViaGen which, for around $50,000, offered to clone pets for owners. The company was a result of a collaboration with the Veterinary Medicine and Biomedical department at Texas A&M University. In 2002, a team from the university created the world's first cloned cat, named CC (which stands for carbon copy), after being approached by a businessman who wanted to clone his dog. No pets had ever been cloned and the man agreed to fund research into the viability of commercial pet cloning.

It took 15 attempts before CC was eventually born. Today the process is much more efficient. CC was created from a cell taken from her big sister, Rainbow. The team then got an egg from an ovary donated by a cat-spaying clinic. The egg was matured in vitro and, using micro-manipulation techniques, its nucleus was removed and replaced with the nucleus from the cell taken from Rainbow. The cell started to divide to create an embryo, which was then implanted in a recipient mother.

Meanwhile CC was still alive and well at 16 years of age and showed no signs of using up any of her nine lives. She'd had a litter of four kittens eleven years ago, one was stillborn, the rest were fit and healthy. They all lived with CC's owner and the man responsible for her creation, Senior Professor Duane Kraemer. She was so unique and valuable that the professor and his wife Shirley built her and her offspring a separate two-storey house with air-con and heating on their ranch. Rainbow had been adopted out, as had the recipient mother. Rainbow died of cancer and the mother was run over by a car. The Kraemers decided that CC and her progeny were too valuable to science to risk and so constructed the cat palace for them.

"She's important and a lot of people are interested in her, so we wanted to have her somewhere people could visit her and she'd be safe," Duane told me when I contacted him. "Some people say she's the best-known and most popular cat in the world. Her story was the biggest story ever out of the University. Her picture was in every newspaper and magazine in the world."

Despite the experimental nature of her creation, CC was remarkably robust and has lived a long, healthy life with hardly any need for veterinary attention. According to Duane, she was "like any other domestic cat."

I asked him about the hypothetical viability of providing cells from Alvin to clone an exact replica. If I wanted Alvin back, could science create him in a test tube? Duane explained that while cloned animals carry the same genes as the animals they are cloned from, those genes are used and expressed in different ways depending on a range of factors.

"As an example, CC has different markings from Rainbow's," he explained. "She hasn't got orange spots like her big sister. It's called epigenetics. Different factors in the DNA will turn genes on and off at different times and create individuals that are different to the ones they are cloned from."

The implications were clear for anyone planning to part with thousands of dollars in the hope of getting a new, exact replica of their beloved pet. There were no guarantees that the clone would even look the same.

"It's like human identical twins: they have the same genes but they still end up being different. The same thing happens with clones. They have the same genes but use them differently for a variety of reasons," explained Duane. "When people call up and say they want their animal cloned I have to assure them that they are not getting their animal back, they are getting a genetic copy that will have differences."

My reactions, of course, were completely natural – sadness and the feelings of loss. People mourn pets, usually just as much as they mourn humans. In 2017 pet insurance company Animal Friends ran a survey that discovered that one in 10 Britons sought counselling or had been prescribed anti-depressants to help them cope with the loss of a pet. In addition, over half of the respondents admitted that the death of their pet made them feel an equal or greater level of sadness as losing a relative. A fifth of pet owners were prepared to pay for a proper pet funeral and a third wanted their pets' body to remain at home with them. The preferred burial site was the back garden. Indeed, Stephanie had buried the body of her previous cat Rocco in the courtyard at the back of her house, which was now rented out to a young couple. She had asked them not to disturb his grave when they moved in.

I thought about my own mum. When her father died, she had helped scatter his ashes behind a rock in the Garden of Remembrance in Garth Road Crematorium in Morden, just down the road from the local waste and recycling centre (she later retrieved them, dried them out on the boiler and shared them out among her siblings). Meanwhile the ashes of her dead Lhasa Apso were afforded slightly more dignity and kept in a custom-made box on a shelf in the kitchen and travelled with her when she emigrated to Australia. The point is, we sometimes seem to have more trouble letting go of our pets than we do of our humans.

My friend Simon similarly cherished the remains of his dogs. Several of them were lined up in oak caskets on his kitchen dresser. It was weird. We let humans go, we put them in holes in the ground, burn them in furnaces and scatter their gritty remnants in fields, under rose bushes and in the ocean. To keep them in urns at home seemed quite creepy to me. I wouldn't want my parents hanging around on the mantelpiece when they go. Yet when it comes to pets, we can't let them go, and this desire to keep their mortal remains in one form or another has led to a booming industry. Several companies will relieve the bereaved of large sums of money to turn their moggy's ashes into diamonds. Taxidermy is also an option. A Dutch artist, Bart Jansen, turned his cat Orville into a drone when it died by having it mounted into a spread-eagle position and attaching motorised propellers to each paw.

Of course, none of these options worked for me because I didn't know if Alvin was dead or alive. Sometimes Stephanie and I would wonder what he was doing. Often the children asked where I thought he might be. But I had nothing except what he'd left behind. Every so often I'd find one of his hairs. Four months passed, then five. Eventually, little by little, the possessions we'd left around the house for when he returned were put in bags and placed in the dark in the cupboard under the stairs where, when he was a kitten, he would find safety and sanctuary. The shelf he curled up on slowly became a little shrine to him. He was a collection of unused toys and bowls and photographs on a phone. His memory lived in the dark with the knick-knacks, blankets and Wellington boots and he remained forever 18 months old, living in the cloud, visiting occasionally when I scrolled through old pictures and videos. Every time I saw him he made me smile.

CHAPTER NINE

LIFE LESS CAT

Alvin had been gone for six months when I stood before the registrar and made my vows to Stephanie.

"I promise to always love and support you… and your cats. Even the ones that will inevitably go missing."

In all the madness and emotions of what was an amazing, beautiful, unconventional day, it was my nod to Alvin (and a chance to get a cheap laugh – I had to take them where I could, given my bride's comedy pedigree). The toast was made to absent friends and cats. We'd talked jokingly in the past of having a cat as a ring-bearer but realised it would be a bad decision on many levels, not least because cats can't be trusted to do as they're told. On the day, we both said how nice it would have been if Alvin was there, we were only half joking. If he hadn't disappeared, he probably would have been brought along in a carrier to make a short guest appearance.

I never proposed to Stephanie. In the summer of 2016, when Alvin was still with us, we had gone on holiday to Italy and driven from Milan in the north to Puglia in the south in a 10-day road trip. We'd often talked around the prospect of marriage but neither of us were particularly into the whistles and bells of it all. One night we were sitting on the promenade in the picturesque seaside town of Otranto, enjoying a few glasses of Chianti and the topic came up.

"What do you think about it?" Stephanie asked.

"I'm not against it," I said honestly, "And I know I want to spend the rest of my life with you. I'm just not into all the ceremony and the pomp."

"If we do it, I'm not doing all the old-fashioned stuff that goes along with it. We go into it as equals. I'm not being given away or walked down the aisle. I'm not having a big dress and not honouring or obeying," she said. "It needs to be fun and relaxed."

We'd both been to too many weddings where the day dragged on and was stifled by convention, bad speeches and enforced dress codes. We decided that the theme for our day would be relaxed fun. We wanted people to laugh.

"So what do you reckon then?" asked Stephanie.

"We might as well do it," I replied.

"When?"

"Next summer?" I offered.

And that was it. That's how we decided to get hitched.

The day was hilarious from beginning to end. We had 70 guests and got married in the barn of a hotel at the foot of Box Hill in Surrey. Stephanie refused to be given away but her lovely father Colin refused not to walk with her down the aisle, so the three of us entered the room together and jostled for space as we walked to the registrar's desk at the front.

We tweaked our vows. I included a mention of cats and a promise to only ever correct Stephanie's grammar silently in my head. Stephanie promised to always laugh at my mishaps.

Later, she topped her own speech off with a fully choreographed comedy interpretative dance routine. Courtesy of my best man Andrew, we even had a video message from TOWIE star Gemma Collins (whose memoirs I ghost-wrote) in which she stated that, if I were ever to become single again, I knew where to find her.

A TALE OF TWO KITTIES

The mention of cats in my vow illustrated just how far I'd gone in my journey. I'd tasted the agony and ecstasy of cat ownership. I'd owned a cat, I'd lost a cat, I'd married a crazy cat lady and I missed cats. Which was how I found myself in a cat café, surrounded by cats that weren't mine, feeling like a recovering alcoholic in a bar, during happy hour.

I went as part of research for a story I was writing on the ubiquity of cats in popular culture and was researching how cats had taken over the internet and were now taking over the high street. Since owning a cat, I had started to pitch more cat-related stories to the newspapers I wrote for. When I stopped to think about it, cats were everywhere. They were in movies, on lunchboxes, on t-shirts, in internet-shared videos and pictures (memes), on social media, and there was a growing number of cat cafés – with eight at the time in the UK. The idea of a cat café is simple. It does what it says on the tin. They are cafés with cats in them. Customers usually book in advance for a specified time slot and can then enjoy tea, coffee, cake and other refreshments while surrounded by the establishment's feline residents. The cats, for their part, seem totally nonplussed by the ebb and flow of human activity.

The best established was Lady Dinah's Cat Emporium in the achingly hip neighbourhood of Shoreditch in the East End of London. The surrounding area was full of quirky businesses: there were beard groomers, quinoa eateries and craft beer micro-breweries with pop-up gin distilleries in the car park. It was hipster heaven and the hottest ticket in town was a Saturday afternoon £10 cake and cuppa at Lady Dinah's where bearded and non-bearded cat lovers sat surrounded by the venue's resident felines. Advance booking was essential and at the most popular times, the 90-minute sessions were booked out weeks in advance.

Lady Dinah's was high-end. In addition to the regular café fare, it also offered a range of afternoon teas including vegetarian, pescatarian and vegan options. The cats lounge around and do their thing. There are no tricks, no shows, no whistles or bells, it was just the people and the cats. The idea behind the cat café phenomenon is that the cats create a calming atmosphere – the cafés are serene places and the languid cats add to the general relaxed feeling. Each cat café has its own set of rules to ensure the welfare of the animals. Certain rules are universal. Flash photography is banned, customers are not allowed to wake sleeping cats and are also discouraged from picking them up. At Lady Dinah's Cat Emporium customers are also asked not to back cats into a corner or crowd them. The animals there have a range of environments and obstacles to enjoy and explore, which are all themed around the idea of an *Alice in Wonderland* Mad Hatter's tea party in an enchanted woodland. There are numerous nooks and crannies for cats to hide in and lounge on and there are also large rotating wheels for the energetic ones to run on. When I was there, most of the cats just slept or wandered around.

As I sat in the quaintly decorated café, I looked around and ruminated. The idea that people would come to a café specifically because it was full of cats would have seemed insane two decades ago. How many bank managers would have loaned money against such a venture? And who would the customers have been? The established image of a cat fanatic had always been the archetypal wild-haired, post-menopausal spinster in a dressing gown who spent her days locked inside an untidy house, surrounded by her furry friends. When I looked around the café, the reality was different. While there were certainly a few women who fitted the description barring the dressing gown, the majority of the clientele was eclectic. There were young and old, families with children (although under 12s were banned) and couples. Most people looked completely normal – apart from one lady in leopard print. I pondered why, when there is no shortage of cats in the UK, so many people would pay money to come and sit in a room full of them? Sure, the coffee and cake was good, but East London had plenty of high-end coffee houses. You couldn't walk more than 50 metres in the neighbourhood without passing somewhere selling cold brew, spirulina-infused soy lattes made with Sumatran coffee beans which had been partially digested and defecated out by live civet cats (because apparently the process imparts a musky smoothness to the resulting coffee).

It wasn't just that corner of London which was cashing in on the cat café trend. There were also similar establishments opening up all over the UK. There was Kitty Café in Nottingham, Maison de Moggy in Edinburgh and the gloriously named Mog on the Tyne in Newcastle. And the craze was international. There were cat cafés all over the world.

The trend began in Taipei, Taiwan in 1998 with the opening of Cat Flower Garden, which quickly became a popular tourist attraction. The idea was taken to Japan, where the first café, Cat's Time, opened in Osaka in 2004. A year later Shop of Cats became the first cat café in Tokyo. Within five years, 79 cat cafés had opened across the country and in just over a decade there were over 35 cafés in Tokyo alone and around 150 across the nation. Japan was the natural launchpad for the idea. The Japanese have a strong affinity with cats – the country is the home of Hello Kitty and it has a national cat day. In the crowded cities many people live in small apartments and are unable to keep their own cats, so the cafés fulfilled a need and became popular with young people.

Wanting to find out more about this surprising trend, I headed to Bristol to meet the owner of a new cat café that was about to open there.

Ewa Rukat, 25, was the brains behind You & Meow. An enterprising businesswoman from Poland, she had raised over £20,000 through crowdfunding and investors to get her idea up and running and was weeks away from opening when I spoke to her. She had previously worked at Lady Dinah's for three years and had been living in Bristol for 18 months when she realised that the city's growing young, urbanite population fitted the customer profile of the London café's clientele.

Modern-day cat cafés tapped into a new, young, social-media hooked population of cat-lovers who shared memes and adored the growing crop of internet-star Instagram cats such as Princess Monster Truck and Nala Cat.

You & Meow was taking bookings before the building work was even finished and before Ewa had any cats.

"I posted a picture of the keys to the property and my Facebook page blew up," she told me. "I was humbled. I knew cat cafés were popular but I had no idea how many cat lovers there were in Bristol. Over 60,000 people got in touch. I didn't even advertise."

Ewa had done her homework. In addition to her time at Lady Dinah's, she had visited every cat café in the UK to research business models. And she knew her market well.

She explained there were two main reasons why people went to cat cafés.

"First, because so many young people now rent and live in cities where landlords won't allow animals. They love cats, but can't own them because they do not own their own homes. When I looked for a location for my café I went to see 22 properties, only three of them would allow me to have cats," she explained.

"Secondly, you look at the most popular content on the internet and it's cats."

She also subscribed to the controversial view that I had come round to – that cats had usurped dogs as man's best friend.

"Young people like cats because they are easier to keep, they are more independent, they are easier to take care of. Dogs are more demanding. They need more space. Cats can be grumpy, but you can leave them when you go to work. They are cooler than dogs," she said.

She was right. Social changes and housing economics mean that Millennials with little hope of owning their own homes, let alone gardens, are also less likely to own dogs. Chihuahuas aside (which seem to be ever more popular with young people), the tide is turning against canines, and cats, with their internet ubiquity and independence, are waiting in the wings, slyly slinking into the space left by dogs. A few dog cafés have also opened, populated by Chihuahuas and other yappy lap dogs, but I imagined they would be a very different proposition, filled with an atmosphere of slobbering excitability.

Even when young people do manage to own their own cats, personal circumstances frequently change and force them to give up their pets. People settle down much later in life and are increasingly mobile, changing jobs and careers and moving around the country, and consequently have to give their cats to rehoming or rescue centres.

"This is very common," said Ewa. "It is sad because you have to give away the animal you love. So for those people who can't have a cat but want to spend time with them, the cafés are a win-win."

For smart cat entrepreneurs setting up cat cafés, welfare must be the primary concern, because stressed cats are prone to disappear and no one wants to be in a cat café where all the cats are grumpy, unengaged or hiding.

"If the cats don't engage with the customers, the customers won't enjoy the experience and won't come back. So it makes business sense to make sure the cats are happy and relaxed," explained Ewa, who planned to fill her café with rescue cats. "You need to love cats too, and have a passion for them, and the house rules are there to protect the cats and ensure their welfare. We always ask customers to behave in a way that doesn't stress the cats."

In addition to the no-flash photography, no waking and no picking up rules, You & Meow customers were forbidden from feeding the cats and were also asked to sanitise hands on arrival. The cats would live in the property, which was linked to 24-hour CCTV so they could be monitored when the café was shut, and every effort was made to ensure their comfort and security.

Despite the popularity of cat cafés, there are concerns about welfare. Ewa certainly cared about the cats that would be living in her premises and they would have all their needs met. However, cat welfare NGO Cats Protection has campaigned against cat cafés, believing there are welfare implications of having a number of cats in a limited space with groups of people unknown to them coming and going throughout the day.

In a statement, it said: "We believe this kind of environment is not suitable for domestic cats because they have evolved as solitary animals and generally do not choose to live in social groups – unlike dogs which are a social species. It is very likely that some or all of the cats involved will become stressed as a result of being in a confined space with a continually changing group of people. This is because domestic cats have shared ancestry with the African wildcat so we still see a lot of these behaviours in our pet cats today. This is not an 'outdated' view – in fact, recent research into cat behaviour counters the opinion that cats living in groups do not suffer social stress."

The cats I saw seemed to be perfectly content and the café owners I spoke to loved and cared for their charges. But it still left questions over whether cafés are the right environments for cats.

***

Our home, meanwhile, seemed empty without a cat in it. We were still stuck in limbo, unsure whether Alvin would ever return, but the longer his disappearance went on, the less likely it seemed. Part of me wanted another, part of me didn't.

Then one day I heard something meowing outside the back door and my heart flipped. I ran to the back of the house and flung open the door expecting to be greeted by Alvin. Instead I looked down and there, sitting on the patio, was the small silver cat that had arrived in the area shortly before Alvin went missing. She was partly to blame.

"Fuck off," I said, slamming the door.

Her name was Rosie, I learned later. She belonged to a family who lived further down the road and had been absent from the neighbourhood for several months because, of all the cats in the area, she'd survived a crossing over the main road but had then been run over on the Esso garage forecourt opposite. She had to have her hips pinned back together again. Despite her possible role in my loss, I had to admire her spirit.

Over the following days she continued to come in the garden and sit by the back door meowing. She was a sweet looking thing, with big eyes and round, chubby cheeks and a snub nose. She was very slight and had striking silver and black markings.

Eventually, I thawed and bent down one afternoon to stroke her. She enjoyed it, purred like a car engine and rubbed her face against my hand. It felt good to have contact with a cat, but at the same time I felt I was betraying Alvin. I knew what was going on. Cats are territorial creatures and have their own spaces. Our garden had been out of bounds all the time we owned a cat, but now he was gone, she was claiming the space as her own. It was a cheek, but it was nature.

She was slightly skittish and jumped when I made sudden moves and then darted off when I stood up, which was probably a hangover from the trauma of being run over. But she returned again and, when the back door was open, she walked in and started sniffing around the house, rubbing her flanks against the furniture to mark her scent, annexing the lounge as brazenly as the Third Reich annexed Austria. I gently picked her up and put her outside.

Her resolve, however, remained undimmed and over the following weeks she returned daily. Eventually, tired of continually removing her from the house, I let her come and go. She was usually after food but I didn't feed her. Her mission was nonetheless complete, and she would turn up most days and hang around the house and garden, often running upstairs to try and get on one of the beds. She must have made a habit of going into other people's houses too because one day I returned home to find a missing leaflet on the doorstep with her face on it. As I was reading it, she appeared outside on the windowsill, peering through the glass at me, meowing to come in. I let her inside and called the neighbours to let them know I had their cat. They explained they wouldn't be back from work for a while so I said I'd keep her in. Finally she got her wish and ran up the stairs and jumped on our bed where she made herself comfortable and fell asleep. Apparently she'd been gone for several days. When her owners came to collect her she was curled up and snoring.

"She hangs around here quite a lot," I tried to explain, feeling guilty. "We try and discourage it but she does manage to get in sometimes."

I couldn't help but see the irony. I had become the sort of person who got attached to other people's cats and, to Rosie's owners, I probably seemed like the lady up the road had seemed to me: a catnapper. Perhaps that's what happened in neighbourhoods with lots of cats, I mused. They changed hands and passed though houses, swapping owners and territories on a whim.

Rosie went home in a carrier and didn't return for a week or so, probably as a result of being kept in. She was a strange cat, with an odd temperament. Sometimes she'd turn up and be affectionate, other times she was nervous, and occasionally she'd hiss aggressively.

As the months went on, Stephanie and I started to discuss getting another cat and we agreed that at some point we would. However, any plans we had were put on hold when we started major building work. For a long time, Stephanie had wanted the old wooden conservatory pulled down and a rear extension erected in its place. I resisted, mainly because I am a man, and so am naturally disinclined to anything that involves fuss and meet change with grumpy reluctance, but also partly because I felt that tearing down the conservatory would in some way be giving up on Alvin. It was his home, after all, and despite the fact that it was decrepit, leaky, leaning to one side and full of gaps between the panels through which you could see daylight, I was sentimental.

"He used to sleep here. If he ever comes back he won't recognise the place," I argued weakly. The building work went ahead anyway. In fairness, it needed to be done and the finished result was well worth all the pain.

The work started in September and took several months. By Christmas 2016 it was nearly finished. We were without a kitchen for many months and lived in dust and noise in the dining room, cooking dinners on a camping stove. It was all quite romantic and old-fashioned. The disruption meant Rosie stayed away and once again, we were a cat-less household, which was unfortunate as by that time, having written several articles about cats for the newspapers I worked with, I was becoming the go-to journalist for cat news. Given my position as cat expert, when I noticed an advert for a cat show in a leisure centre just a few miles from home, I decided to investigate further and learn about the world of cat fancying. I was totally unprepared for what I discovered.

CHAPTER TEN
BEST IN SHOW

The London Cat Show – or LondonCats (all one word, because it is cool) was where the dreams and aspirations of 220 cats and kittens were either realised or crushed by a panel of 15 international cat judges. And all the drama went on just 10 minutes away from where I lived in the inauspicious surroundings of Leatherhead Leisure Centre. Like most normal people, I had never been to a cat show in my life. I didn't even know such a thing existed until I'd researched it.

My initial hope that the show would include disciplines such as cat agility tests and choreographed dance routines between owners and their moggies was dashed when Steven Meserves, event organiser and consequently the man in charge of the image of cat fancying in the UK, explained that cats can't dance.

Steven was an affable PR company owner originally from Boston in the US, who also happened to own the world's highest-ranking show kitten, an American shorthair called Mowgleaves Stonehenge (Mowgleaves being the breeder name, Stonehenge because he is British).

He got his first cat after he answered a newspaper ad in the US selling "toy leopards" at the age of 18. The cat he bought was one of the first Bengals to be bred – he owned one before they were a recognised breed. After that he became hooked.

Like Ewa the cat café owner, he believed cats were in the ascendency. He'd seen hard evidence while promoting the show at the UK's first cat all-nighter, a nightclub cat-themed festival where cat video clips were played to pounding dance music for young hedonists.

"It was a 10pm to 6am party with 4,000 people. It was crazy," he said. "If you think about it, it makes complete sense. Look at all the YouTube videos and the memes. People love cats and there is a new generation of internet-savvy, connected young people who are seriously into them."

I learned that in the UK, there are two official cat-fancying bodies. LondonCats was organised by The International Cat Association, or TICA. They were the young upstarts who were new in the UK but staged 10,000 shows a year across the world in countries including China, Russia and the US, where shows could attract up to 5,000 people. TICA was intent on shaking up the fusty image of cat fancying and introducing it to a new, young, family-orientated audience. Around 2,000 people were expected to visit LondonCats and many of them would be hip youngsters, following in the footsteps of cat-owning celebrity standard-bearers such as Ed Sheeran, Zayn Malik, Russell Brand, Taylor Swift and Christopher Walken. And who was in the dog corner? Ben Fogle and Paul O'Grady!

At the other end of the UK cat show spectrum was the more traditional Governing Council of the Cat Fancier (GCCF), which was the older UK organisation. Steven was kind about the competition and didn't once mention the phrase "crazy cat ladies".

TICA was progressive and ambitious, Steven explained to me, with plans to become as big as the London Pet Show, but just for cats.

"We are slowly morphing into a cooler hobby," Steven explained. "The crazy cat lady stigma is going. Don't get me wrong, they are still around, but we are seeing more professional people getting interested because cats are easier to have than dogs, they require less maintenance and you can have them in towns and cities." He admitted, however, that he did encounter a slight disconnect between his day job in fashion PR, and his passion for felines.

"Presently, at work, I am organising a Vivienne Westwood fashion show," he told me. "People ask me what I'm doing at the weekend and I would like one day not to have to be so coy about saying I'm going to a cat show."

The more I learned, the more I could see how cats could be cool. In addition to household moggies and the more traditional pedigree breeds such as Siamese and Persian, there were the exotic "hybrid breeds" such as Bengals and Savannahs, which resulted from crossing domestic cats with wild cats and were being developed all the time. The LondonCats show was going to be the debut event at which the newest exotic was unveiled. The Marguerite – the result of crossing a domestic cat with an African Sand Cat – had never been shown before. It was small, compact, squat and muscular with small features and a cute, inquisitive expression that belied its heritage. African sand cats are some of the most hardy wildcats in the world, adapted to living in deserts in temperatures ranging from -5°C to 52°C. Pound for pound, they have one of the strongest bites of any feline and hearing far more sensitive than any domestic cat. The first Marguerites were bred by Jacky and Tim Bliss, a husband and wife duo who specialised in breeding exotics and who held a dangerous animal licence at their cattery and breeding centre in

Lincolnshire. The first generation were sired from a captive bred Sand Cat named Trevor.

Another curiosity at LondonCats was the Lykoi, or werewolf cat, which due to a genetic mutation looks like something from a horror movie. The mutation causes the cats to have no undercoat and their hair appears coarse and thin. They also have angular faces, adding to their odd appearance. Dermatologists at the University of Texas examined a Lykoi for skin abnormalities and discovered that some hair follicles lacked the necessary components required to create hair, hence no undercoat. They also found that the follicles that were able to produce hair lacked the ability to maintain the hair, which is why Lykoi moult and can become almost completely bald from time to time.

These weird and wonderful creatures were at the cutting edge of domestic feline evolution and TICA recognised over 50 cat breeds.

My first taste of cat fancying was both a strange and fun experience. The main hall of the leisure centre had become a cat carnival where row upon row of competitors sat and stood next to large canvass tents and metal pens inside which lounged cats by the score, of every conceivable size and shape, waiting to be judged. There were five categories, including two for household moggies. Pedigrees were scored on specific breed characteristics such as ear and eye shape and at the end of the weekend, the cat or kitten with the highest overall score was named Best in Show.

I chatted to Steven and found out more about his life.

"I'm 42 now but I've been doing this since I was 18," he said. "I used to put on huge shows in Madison Square Gardens. I've been trying to show the public over here that we're not just crazy people who prance our cats around. This is a legit thing."

"You're rebranding cats," I said.

"I'm trying to," he laughed. "Come and meet Stone."

He took me to a quiet corner of the main hall to a line of show tents. Stone, the world's best kitten, was relaxing inside one. Steven reached in and pulled him out.

"Have a hold," he offered.

I took him from Steven and was amazed by his weight. He was incredibly dense and muscly, and totally different from what I was used to. Alvin was thin and lithe, scrawny almost. In contrast Stone was the cat equivalent of an athlete. And he was impeccably behaved. He was happy being handled, he didn't flinch or squirm. His coat was silky soft and groomed to perfection.

"He's beautiful," I cooed.

We replaced Stone in his pen and I took a wander around the show. It was frenetic, with a big, mixed crowd meandering along the rows of competitors. Each breed and category had its own row: the Sphinx and Siamese were in one, the ragdolls and gigantic Maine Coons, some as big as medium-sized dogs, were in another. Every few minutes announcements came over the tannoy and a flurry of owners grabbed their cats and took them to the judges, while others returned to their stations where cats were preened and fed, ready for the next round. To get through the crowds, owners had to hoist their animals aloft and call, "Cat coming through." The whole spectacle was bizarre.

I made my way down the exotics aisle and got talking to a man from Norway who explained more about the art of breeding hybrids. He told me that a breeder needed to produce seven generations of lineage from the original wild to domestic union before a cat was considered domesticated enough to be a normal house cat. The first generation, the direct result of a mating between a wildcat and domestic cat, was classed as an F1. These kittens would be 50 per cent wild blood. They would then be mated again to produce F2 and so on until F7, which would ideally retain the wild markings and appearance of their forebears, but with none of the bite.

The man explained that he bred Savannahs, which were hybrids between domestic cats and Servals, another type of wildcat. He told me that some of his cats were so long, when they stood on their hind legs their paws came up to his shoulder, and he was a tall bloke.

"Aren't they dangerous?" I asked.

He assured me they had calm temperaments.

"The Savannahs are fine," he said, "but I also breed Bengals and they are the ones you need to watch. They are very lively cats."

I rubbed the old scars on my wrist from Alvin's playful kitten days.

We talked about the difficulties and controversies that breeders at the cutting edge of new breed creation experienced, particularly when dealing with wild cats. He told me that not so long ago in Norway, a captive-bred Serval which wasn't properly licensed came to the attention of the authorities. Servals are dangerous wild animals and have to be kept in strict conditions. The Norwegian authorities couldn't find a home for the animal so decided to destroy it. In the UK, Jacky and Terry Bliss (who bred the first Marguerites) heard about the case and attempted to save the animal and bring it over here. They built a suitable enclosure to keep it in and liaised with Defra (Department for Rural Affairs and Agriculture) to make sure all the relevant permissions were in place. Despite their efforts, the cat was destroyed by the Norwegians anyway.

"Why did they kill it?" I asked.

The man shrugged.

"There is so much red tape and paperwork and nothing is joined up. In the end it's the animals that suffer," he said. It seemed particularly unfair, given the efforts that had been made to save it.

The world of pedigree breeding is not without its critics. Animals are selectively bred to bring out certain characteristics. Mainly, in the case of cats, and to some degree dogs, breeds are developed for a certain look. Bengals were developed for their leopard-like spotted coats, Maine Coons for their size, Ragdolls for their appearance and gentle placid temperaments. In some cases those physical characteristics affect the health of the animals in potentially adverse ways. Bengals can be prone to heart conditions, eye diseases and joint problems, Maine Coons are prone to cardiomyopathy, hip problems and spinal muscular atrophy, Ragdolls to bladder stones. Rex cats are specifically bred to have curly fur and this selective breeding has led to specific health issues, including Devon Rex spasticity (also called hereditary myopathy). This condition makes muscles weak and is eventually fatal. It seemed that the cats sometimes paid a heavy price for the genetic manipulation that created them. This was the less talked about aspect of pedigree breeding and led me to wonder about the ethics of the process. It was a moral maze and one that, when widened, can lead to questions about dog breeding and any animal breeding programmes.

Like cat cafés, the issue of commercial breeders has been raised by Cats Protection, which wants better safeguards for the commercial sale of all types of cats. It's estimated that only 10 per cent of cats are pedigrees, and the charity is concerned about those that are repeatedly bred for sale irresponsibly. However, it does acknowledge that there are responsible sellers and that good practice and high welfare standards exist, "particularly within membership organisations".

At LondonCats, none of the pampered and mollycoddled moggies seemed neglected or ill-treated. And for show cat owners with the top kitties, it was not a cheap hobby and there were few rewards. Those who competed internationally had to factor in the cost of air travel, hotels, car hire and cat care. Top cats ate diets of specially made raw food. The only money to be made was from stud cats and litters. A normal kitten from a pedigree breeder can sell for around £1,500 but breeding champions are worth much more. A top male with all his bits intact can sell for around £3,000 to £5,000.

Steven told me that in the previous year he'd spent £25,000 travelling around the world with Stone. "It could be worse. I could have a drug habit," he shrugged.

For UK cat fanciers, international travel is doubly hard because of stricter rules on animal movements. Only certain UK airlines will carry cats, dogs and ferrets in the hold as cargo and there is a long list of regulations and requirements that must be met before an animal can get airborne. Animals must be microchipped, vaccinated against rabies and need to have the correct paperwork. Some airlines run their own pet cargo services and there are also independent carriers that specialise in flying pets around the world. None of this matters, however, if you want to take your cat or dog into or out of the

UK on a plane in the cabin with you, because the UK authorities will not allow it. The only exceptions are assistance animals such as guide dogs, which are allowed in the cabin as long as they meet the airlines requirements and are fully trained. Some airlines will also accept emotional support animals into cabins, although this is more of a grey area.

Emotional support animals are used in therapy to improve social, emotional and cognitive conditions in patients, and certain airlines, mainly in the US, will allow them to travel with their owners on flights in the cabin if the owner has a psychiatrist's letter confirming the need for the animal. Emotional support animals are predominantly cats and dogs but there have also been parrots, lizards, monkeys, horses, dolphins and elephants, most of which would present an airline with logistical headaches, not least in the case of the elephant and dolphin. However, emotionally supportive pigs, marmosets and turkeys have all been allowed on flights with their anxious owners.

In one case I found, an American named Carla Fitzgerald who developed PTSD after being in a car accident in 2013 was allowed to fly with her emotional support duck named Daniel Turducken Stinkerbutt. He wore a harness and red booties when he travelled. Another woman attempted to take an emotional support peacock on a United Airlines flight but was less lucky and was refused permission. In recent years, several airlines have tightened the rules on emotional support animals following a rise in on-board incidents including urination, biting and defecation – none of which one imagines would do anything to ease the anxieties of the animals' owners.

While pets are not allowed in the cabins of planes departing and arriving the UK, it is a different story on the Continent, where some airlines will allow passengers to take animals under a certain weight in the cabin as hand luggage. KLM, for example, allows pets in a travel case up to a maximum of 8kg. Consequently, when Steven, who lived in London, travelled to a show abroad he usually took a train to Harwich, a ferry to the Hook of Holland, another train to Amsterdam and then a flight to wherever the show was. Stone travelled in a carry case with him.

So why did he do it?

"It's expensive and there is not much glamour. If Stone wins it validates my efforts. It's the competition, but it's also a hobby. I get to travel all over the world, and I have friends everywhere," he answered. "You could make money selling kittens, but for most of us that's not the driving goal. Breeding a cat of such quality brings a huge sense of accomplishment."

I was fascinated by the competitive element of the cat-fancying world. Events are co-ordinated and cats accumulate scores through the show season, which runs each year from May to April. The scoring system is complex: show cats get points not only for their characteristics and appearance but also for the other cats they beat. It was like a feline version of Pokémon crossed with Top Trumps. Owners could be incredibly strategic about which shows they entered, sometimes choosing smaller shows which high-ranking cats would be taking part in, in the knowledge that if they won, they would get more points than they would in a bigger show with fewer high-ranking cats.

Steven mentioned that with just a few months to go until the end of the season, Stone was in contention to become the best show cat in the world in both the adult and kitten category because during the season, Stone had turned 10 months, which according to the regulations was when a kitten can compete as an adult. There was just one other serious competitor in the adult section. The following weekend Steven planned to take Stone to a small show in Italy where there were easy points to be won, while the other cat was going to a show in the USA. If his strategy worked, it would boost Stone's chances of overall victory.

"Who is the other cat?" I asked.

"His father," said Steven, "he's a Russian."

It was like a 1980s Hollywood drama: two opponents locked in combat from different sides of the ideological divide but bonded by blood. From the Space Race to the arms race, from politics to sport, East and West have long been locked in epic rivalry. But not since Rocky Balboa stepped into the ring with Ivan Drago in *Rocky IV* had there been a Cold War head-to-head as explosive as the one playing out internationally in cat shows across the world that year.

While Mowgleaves Stonehenge was the young Anglo-American upstart from London, the title holder in the red corner was Rumfold Such A Flirt Shu-Ko, the Beast from the East and pride of Moscow, also nicknamed Sashock. He hailed from the cattery of legendary Russian cat breeder Nadejda Rumyantseva. And in a twist worthy of a Star Wars storyline, Sashock had sired Stone, as Steven and Nadejda were friends who knew each other.

"The Russian is quite a pretty cat," admitted Steven. "But Stone only has four shows as an adult under his belt so to be as highly ranked as he is currently is really impressive. He's already in first place in the kitten category and is holding strong there. The same cat has never won kitten and adult in the same year and you only get one shot so I'm going for it!"

The cats themselves had never actually met despite frequently being in the same venue.

"They don't mix at shows," said Steven. "It's not that they wouldn't get on, it is just that people are paranoid because cats can pick up infections from other cats, so they are all kept apart."

I was intrigued to learn more about these two cats and after the show I contacted Nadeja. Although Stone was an America Shorthair, Nadeja's expertise was in breeding Scottish Folds and Scottish Straights. Sashock was a Scottish Fold, a breed distinguished by their novel downturned ears, which give them an owl-like appearance. The ear shape is the result of a cartilage weakness that can cause cats that haven't been carefully bred to have knee problems.

Nadeja, a registered breeder since 1993, learned about the peculiarities and difficulties of stock breeding Scottish Folds from a woman called Nina Popova, who was the first to breed them in Russia. When Nina died in 2006, Najeda took most of the prized cats from her cattery.

I spoke to Najeda while she was in Singapore giving a grooming presentation. In addition to being a legendary breeder, she also had her own range of cat shampoos, grooming products, and grooming salons. She was also an expert in breeding genetics and gave regular seminars on the subject. She pinpointed South East Asia as the most cat-loving region she worked in. In Thailand, for example, people will do anything for cats, including massage and spa treatments. They will even hire personal cat nannies, groomers and doctors, she explained.

In Russia her cattery was in the countryside to the east of Moscow. Her Scottish Fold bloodline was arguably the most sought-after in the world and her breeding operation was run with regimented Soviet-style efficiency. She told me she refused to work with other Russian breeders as many are unethical.

"I have the biggest cattery in Europe but not all my cats live with me," she said in a thick Russian accent. "I have staff who care for them 24 hours a day. In my home, I have around 25 adults and 40 kittens. This is not too much. I have eight co-owners who have my breeding females and males and help me make my breeding programme."

She also had an agent in France who sometimes took Sashock to European shows for her.

She explained that she was intent on winning the season. I asked about her tactics.

"We can only win at big shows with a high point count. We have to plan it very well. Ultimately it is a cat, not a toy and I don't want him to become tired. If he has two or three weeks' break between shows he feels perfect," she explained. "Competition this year is interesting. I hope we keep our place. I will keep my fingers crossed for Russia but America is catching up. Russia is proud of my cat but as Steven's cat was born from my boy it doesn't matter who is first or second. It is a good result either way."

Stone and Sashock were due to come face to face again twice at shows in France before the end of the season, which would decide the final placings.

Several weeks after LondonCats I caught up with Steven. His gamble had paid off. "The Russian" had been to a big show in Oregon in the US along with several of the other cats in the top 10. They all cancelled each other out because they split the judge's votes and shared the points. Steven went to a lesser known show near Milan with Stone, where there were still around 75 other cats but where Stone had a much better chance of picking up points.

It was like the Formula One, with constant interchanges between the top competitors for the remainder of the season. Ultimately, however, Sashock had built up enough of a buffer to finally see off the newcomer when the season ended. Rumfold Such A Flirt Shu-ko was crowned TICA adult cat of the year 2017, while Mowgleaves Stonehenge came second in the adult section, but won best kitten of the year.

CHAPTER ELEVEN

BENGAL FULL THROTTLE

A year had passed since Alvin disappeared and, after my experiences in the quirky world of cat fancying, I was itching to get a moggy. Seeing the different cats had made me realise how much I missed having a cat around the house and that moggies were pretty cool.

I wasn't naive enough to think that Alvin could be replaced, but I missed his character and wondered whether it would be possible to find an equally characterful cat. The final deciding factor was the mice. The builders had gone and the construction work had obviously disturbed a legion of rodents that had been quietly living under the house minding their own business. We were overrun. Before all the floors and skirting boards were sealed up and finished, they rose from the foundations and scurried out from gaps in a tide of squeaking fur. They scampered through the kitchen and crapped in the new units in the utility room. Some of them were bold and didn't even bother to hide when a human walked in the room, they just squatted on their haunches, whiskers twitching, squinting through their beady little black lifeless eyes. I bought traps. They were useless against such numbers. The mice just helped themselves to the bait food, which they managed to eat without triggering the devices. I called in a pest controller who arrived looking like he'd just walked out of the pages of a Dickens novel. He had a thin crescent-shaped face with sharp features and a long chin full of stubble. He wore a flat cap, a dusty old jacket and fingerless gloves. He threw scoops of poison-laden grain behind and under the kitchen units and said that he wasn't supposed to use so much but that if we wanted the problem to go away, it was the best solution.

"The final solution," he cackled.

Still the mice came. Eventually they managed to get upstairs too and must have been crawling through the walls. They ate a hole in one of my backpacks. They gnawed into the kids' soft toys. They stripped the feathers from one of Stephanie's favourite dress jackets.

One night, half asleep, I heard a noise coming from the corner of the room. I thought I was dreaming that Alvin was back. The next morning, I discovered a shredded chocolate wrapper in the bin and a tiny mouse turd.

They invaded the storage shed outside and ate their way through my inflatable dingy, causing hundreds of pounds of damage. That was the last straw. I loved that boat and had spent many happy hours puttering up and down the Thames in it.

"We're getting a cat," I told Stephanie in a complete reversal of the conversation we'd had two and a half years previously. She took less persuading than I had.

"Okay," she said.

The only contentious issue was my choice of breed.

"We're getting a Bengal," I said. "A proper one this time. Full throttle, no messing around."

I surveyed the ruins of my boat and plucked a single desiccated mouse corpse from the fist-sized hole chewed in it. The rodent had either died of plastic poisoning or had become trapped inside the rigid rubber tomb.

"I want a cat that's going to rip these little bastards to pieces," I scowled as held up the tiny flat body. It was war and I needed to wheel out the big guns.

Stephanie wasn't so sure.

"Any cat will get rid of mice," she said. "Once the mice smell that there's a cat in the house, they'll go away." She was right, as usual. A cat is an effective deterrent whether it hunts mice or not. Mice have evolved receptors that detect specific proteins in their predators' saliva and urine and cause them to feel fear.

But I wasn't interested. I wanted bloody retribution and I was certain that a Bengal, with its leopard cat hybridity, would do the trick.

"Cry havoc! And let slip the cats of war," I announced dramatically, kicking the crumpled boat before walking off to look for Bengal cats for sale on Gumtree.

I knew a bit about the breed from the rudimentary research I'd done when we got Alvin and from the discussions I'd had with breeders at LondonCats. I recalled the Norwegian gentleman who told me that Bengals could be demanding pets. I was unperturbed. I wanted a cat with character, pluck and courage. I wanted a spotted warrior. Naively, given my newly acquired knowledge of the hybrid cat breeding process, I didn't realise that aside from early-generation, semi-wild crossbreeds, the wild character-istics of leopard cats are bred out of domestic Bengals and all that remains are the markings. They are designed to be pleasant and trustworthy family companions. They are sheep in wolves' – or leopard's – clothing.

The popularity of the Bengal as a household pet grew in the 1980s, but records of wildcat and domestic hybrids date back to 1871, when reports show that novel breeds were among the attractions at the first organised cat show, which was held in Crystal Palace in London. Before this seminal event in cat-fancying history, moggies had largely been kept as pest controllers and by and large were badly treated and tolerated only as long as they kept vermin under control. Prior to the show, Victorians would never have dreamt of cuddling or grooming their cats. However, even though only just over 50 cats were shown at the event, it was so novel that it sparked an interest in cats and cat shows. By 1885 the craze had spread to the US, where there are records of a cat show being held in Madison Square Gardens. In 1887 the National Cat Club was formed and its first show attracted 320 cats. Photographs from 1900 show upper-class women exhibiting cats on leads at another show in the Royal Botanic Gardens, Kew.

Interest continued to grow and breeders tried to develop new, exotic bloodlines. There are reports of attempts to cross Asian leopard cats with domestic cats in Belgium in 1934 and in Japan in 1941.

The first recorded deliberate cross of a tomcat with a leopard cat dates from 1963, according to the *New York Times*, which identifies Californian cat fanatic Jean Mill as the breeder. Jean, who studied genetics, is known in cat-fancying circles as the queen of the Bengals and she is supposed to have created the hybrid in an attempt to save populations of wild leopard cats which were trapped and killed for their attractive fur. Jean figured that if she could create a domestic cat that looked like a leopard, rich fur-wearing women would want to own one and be less inclined to wear one.

In the 70s on the US East Coast, zookeeper and exotic cat peddler Bill Engler also established a wildcat hybrid breeding programme. He imported and sold small wildcats and noticed that supply was drying up, so set about creating "a small exotic cat that was beautiful, had the disposition that was suitable for a pet house cat, a greater resistance to disease of civilization than his jungle-bred cousins, and that would readily reproduce himself." He is credited with coming up with the name Bengal. Some say the name was taken from the leopard cat's Latin name, *felis bengalensis*, while others say the name was self-referential – B Engler. Bill was a member of the Long Island Ocelot club and in 1972 he shared his vision with fellow members, telling them: "We are all aware of the increasing difficulty in getting, as well as the increasing costs of ocelots, puma and other exotics we love. I hope that these Bengals can not only help fill the gap between the supply and demand for exotics, but help to create greater interest in all exotics, that this interest be beneficial in funding research for production of and legislation for the protection of all the cats." In 1975, Bill claimed to have produced over 60 Bengals.

The Bengal has a chequered history in the cat-fancying world. Initially Jean was met with opposition, as most breeders were against breeding a wild cat with a domestic. She ploughed on but came across a hurdle when she discovered that most of the males from the early Bengal litters were sterile. She needed a suitable male cat to cross with her fertile female hybrids and legend has it that she eventually found one living on its own in the rhinoceros enclosure at New Delhi Zoo in India. The leopard-like feral cat was most likely the result of a domestic and wild cat pairing in the wild. Jean managed to secure it for her breeding programme and it handled the task with enthusiasm.

First generation hybrids are a handful and not suitable as household pets as they are 50 per cent wild. In Britain, the first generation of savannah cats, for example, can only be kept under licence and in outdoor cages, in accordance with the Dangerous Wild Animals Act (DWAA). Early generation Bengals should only be homed by experienced owners. In the US, you needed a licence to keep one up until 2007 when the rules were changed. By the fourth-generation stage, or F4, Bengals have usually lost any wild instincts. For many years, however, the fancying community were wary. As Jean Mill once said: "Any other cat can bite a judge and excuses are made, but if a Bengal bites they claim it's the wild blood. Our Bengals must be the sweetest cats at the cat show." (Her words would come back to haunt me.)

Most of the breeders I spoke to kept their cats indoors. There are pros and cons. Many say that if a cat has always been a house cat, it knows no different and isn't bothered about going out. Others say it's in a cat's nature to want to roam and that they should be free. As I was looking for a suitable pet, the in or out debate became contentious.

"I don't think I could bear it if we got another cat and it went missing." Stephanie told me. "It will have to stay inside. How would you feel if it got snatched or lost?"

"It's in a cat's nature to want to roam. You can't keep them inside," I argued.

"But if it doesn't go outside, it will never know the difference."

"It's not fair on the cat to deny it the right to go outside," I countered.

Stephanie suggested a compromise. "It can go outside, but we can train it on a harness and take it for walks."

"That's not the answer. Cats need freedom." I was adamant.

We had many discussions and eventually found a solution. We would investigate the possibility of erecting a cat-proof fence around the garden, so the cat could go outside and have some freedom, but not too much. I was unsure, but figured it would still have to be inside for six months and during that time I could work on another plan of action.

Bengals, it turned out, were not in short supply and it took a lot of research and phone calls to sort out the dodgy dealers and the chancers who were trying to pass off tabby cats as Bengals from the genuine ones. We tried several rehoming services first, but Bengals went almost immediately. Eventually we found a registered breeder in Leamington Spa who had recently had a Bengal litter to a prize-winning father and had one cat left, a male. She sent photos and, on a crisp February morning in 2017, a few days before Stephanie's birthday, we drove to meet her. I was actually excited at the prospect. Even though we hadn't agreed and wanted to see the cat and its mother and the type of conditions it was bred in first, I knew that if it all squared up, we'd be returning home with a kitten. And, just in case, I went out to the pet shop before we left and bought high-end, high meat content food, treats, toys, a bowl, a bed and a litter tray.

On the way we had the name discussion.

"He's exotic, so it's got to be something that sounds ridiculous," I said. "Ian? Kevin?"

We batted some names around.

Then Stephanie said: "Barry. Barry the Bengal."

We both laughed. Barry was perfect.

The-kitten-who-would-potentially-be-named-Barry lived on a smallholding at the end of the residential road on the outskirts of town. The house looked ramshackle from the outside and there were outbuildings scattered around. In one, there were enclosures with puppies in them.

We were met by a middle-aged woman who looked like she embraced the outdoor life. She showed us to a brick conservatory at the back of the house where the kitten was living with its mother. There was a bed for them, a bowl of food and water and little else, apart from a table, some sacks of food and a drain. The mother looked fit and healthy and the kitten was adorable and full of life. It was not nervous and trotted over to see us. The woman explained that the kitten's brother had been picked up the day before and taken to a new home in Liverpool, which Stephanie found fitting. I explained that if we took it, the last kitten would be getting the better deal because he was coming to the south where the warmer climate would be much more in keeping with his Asian ancestry. We both bent down to offer a hand and the kitten sniffed and started licking. His tiny rough tongue was like a minute wet cheese grater. I stood up and continued talking to the woman and the cat jumped on my leg and clung on with his tiny claws, just as Alvin had done when we first met.

"He wants to come home with us," I laughed. Given the sparseness of his surroundings I think maybe he did. He clung on for ages and climbed higher, so I reached down and picked him up and he started licking me again. At the other end of the outhouse, the mother started mewling. She'd lost the rest of her litter and she knew what was coming next. I felt that familiar twinge of guilt and looked at her apologetically. The kitten didn't seem too bothered though. I like to think that Barry knew what side his bread was buttered, saw the nice people who had come to meet him, looked around at his surroundings and decided he was coming home with us. We didn't really have to make a decision, he decided for us and cold-shouldered his mother with heartless indifference.

After a quick conflab with the owner, we agreed on the sale and I endeavoured to get the dirty business of taking a small creature from its mother over as swiftly as possible. I ran to the car to get the carrier and steeled myself for the drive home, during which I feared Barry would realise what had happened and start wailing, much as Alvin had done years previously.

We got his papers, which we could register him with if we chose, and gently placed him in the carrier. He was as light as a feather, fragile and precious. Once again, as I had felt with Alvin, I was quite disgusted with myself because I was complicit in an abduction, but this time I was excited as well. The mother let out a mournful, throaty cry. Like a coward I left Stephanie to hand over the money, made my excuses and scarpered to the car with the furry spoils. I strapped the carrier into the back seat and reflected on my own self-loathing.

Stephanie followed and I got in the driving seat and gunned the engine.

"I feel awful," I said. "It's not nice taking something away from its birth mother, even if we are going to give it a better home in a nicer place. Imagine how Madonna feels," I joked.

We talked gently to Barry as we drove back through the town to try and get him used to our voices and to calm him. He must be terrified and confused, I thought. He let out a couple of weak meows and then fell silent.

"Is he okay?" I frowned. I knew about the congenital heart problems some pedigree cats suffer and worried that the shock had sent him into cardiac arrest. I couldn't see him in the back. Stephanie leaned over the passenger seat to check.

"I think he's asleep," she said.

And he was. Barry the Bengal was so nonplussed about being torn from the bosom of his mother, he'd dropped off. He slept all the way back on the two-hour journey and only roused himself when the car stopped outside the back of the house in the dark. We carried him inside, opened the carrier and let him come out in his own time. He didn't need any coaxing. He strode out, head high, ears twitching and started to explore the surroundings. There were no nerves and no apprehension. He wandered from room to room, then found his food bowl and started to eat.

In the light I got a proper look at him. He had beautiful markings and looked both exotic, wild and ridiculously cute. His nose and mouth were white and his button nose was rose pink. His back and flanks were a patchwork of stripes, spots and rosettes. He was a mix of light brown hues and his tummy was soft cream with black spots. His eyes were wide and inquisitive. There were lines around them that tapered together into a single line above his cheek. The patterns gave him an Egyptian look. On his chest there was a distinctive W-shaped black collar that made it appear as if he was wearing a ruff. When he sat upright, he looked regal, like a little Pharaoh. He was vocal too, with a full repertoire of purrs, squeaks and tiny meows.

Once he'd settled we went in to the lounge and left him to explore on his own. He'd had a long day and we didn't want to crowd him. He sniffed around and followed us. We sat down on the sofa and he tried to join us, but was too small to manage the jump, so he sat by our feet meowing. I reached down and lifted him up and he climbed over us and the pillows, sniffing out and investigating every corner. We discussed sleeping arrangements and decided that this time there would definitely be no cats in the bedroom. From day one, Barry was going to learn that he could have the run of the house except the main bedroom. I had given in to Alvin and eventually capitulated and let him in the bedroom, but this time I vowed things would be different. Barry was going to learn his place. He had his litter tray and a nice new comfy bed. There was no reason he needed to be in with us. I also wanted him to stay downstairs to sort out any mice that appeared.

By bedtime, Barry had started to wane. He grew tired and clumsy and although he was still intrigued by his new surroundings, he was having trouble keeping his eyes open. I picked him up, took him to his bed and said goodnight. He didn't stay put for long, however, and followed me to the bottom of the stairs. He had obviously never seen this new obstacle before and sat at the bottom looking up at me, with an alarmed look on his face.

I shrugged back at him and apologised but was resolute. He'd just have to learn his place. He was here to do a job. He was our mouser and he needed to stay downstairs and get acquainted with the enemy.

I felt slightly guilty getting into bed that first night and I could hear his little cries from the bottom of the stairs, but I put in some earplugs to drown out the noise and fell asleep.

The following morning, we both got up early, excited to see him and a little apprehensive in case there had been any nocturnal damage or defecation. Downstairs there was no sign of Barry. We looked in every room and called for him. For a moment there was panic. What if he'd got himself wedged in some corner or had found a way out? Then I heard a rustling noise coming from the cupboard under the stairs and as I looked, a furry little body slid out from the gap under the door. Like Alvin before him, Barry found sanctuary in the dark. It must have been uncomfortable as there were was no bedding in there, so we put a blanket down for him in case he was going to make a habit of sleeping there, which he did. The cupboard became Barry's den too. Whenever we went out, he was always there when we came back. He'd crawl out from under the door, yawn and bound over for a stroke and an ear scratch. I looked forward to seeing him. It was a stark contrast to the early days when Alvin had come home with us and I was full of reluctance and allergies.

***

I didn't tell the children we were getting another kitten as I wanted to surprise them and when they came to stay a couple of days after he arrived, we walked indoors and I told them to have a look in the cupboard under the stairs. They opened it and there he was, curled up on his blanket, blinking.

Millie couldn't contain herself and cried. Lucas took one look at him and asked: "Is he a Bengal?"

When I told him yes, he sighed and, haunted by the memory of his exchanges with Alvin, said, "Great, that's my life over then!"

I assured him that if he exerted his place in the pack and showed no fear, Barry would learn to respect him.

Barry was a noisy little ball of energy and explored everything. He grew quickly and within a week had worked out how to get up the stairs, taking each one at a time, leaping up step by step, pulling himself up by his front legs when he couldn't jump high enough. He discovered the bedroom and the bed, which he managed to climb onto in the same determined manner. His energy levels were limitless. He careered around the house, climbing, jumping and scratching his way over people and furniture.

Like Alvin, he took a shine to mouse-shaped toys, which I took as a good sign. One in particular became a firm favourite. It had a small rattle inside. Barry would toss it around and tumble over it in a play-battle. One day he trotted up to me with the toy in his mouth. He looked like a dog bringing a stick to its owner. He dropped it at my feet, looked up at me and let out a little squeak. I raised an eyebrow.

"What do you want?"

He squeaked again so I picked up the toy by its tail and waved it around in front of him. He batted it with his front paws and after a few seconds of sparring, I let him have it. He threw it around, then picked it up, walked a few steps towards me and dropped it at my feet again, gazing up expectantly.

"What? Do you want me to throw it for you?"

I'd heard that Bengals like to play fetch but didn't really believe it.

I picked up the mouse and threw it across the room. Barry bounded off after it. Leapt on it, threw it around and then brought it back in his mouth and dropped it by my feet. I laughed and threw it again. The game lasted about 15 minutes until he got bored. Each time he brought the mouse back and dropped it at my feet, then waited for me to throw it again.

I showed Stephanie.

"He's like a dog," she laughed.

He was. He loved playing fetch, he was inquisitive, gregarious and remarkably sociable. He followed me everywhere, demanding my attention. He wanted to play all the time. When I tried to work, he jumped onto the desk top, clambered over the keyboard and sat directly in front of the monitor to obscure my view. He looked at me, pleading. If I ignored him, he walked back and forth brushing against the monitor, which was touchscreen. It became difficult to get anything done.

He loved to climb, particularly up legs. When our builder Jon came round, Barry took a liking to him too, and began launching himself playfully at his legs. Jon, a strapping six-footer, cowered from him.

One afternoon I heard meowing by the back patio doors and saw Rosie crouching outside, begging to come in. She hadn't been around for several months and I suspected she'd had another mishap on the road. She'd put on weight and looked grubby. I called Barry. I wanted her to realise that there was a new cat in town and the house and garden were no longer her domain. Barry sauntered over to the doors, which were slightly raised from the patio outside, and looked down at this strange interloper. She looked startled, and then affront-ed. Who was this newcomer? She began to emit a low, guttural moan, which ascended several octaves and finished in a howl. It was an expression of cat envy. Barry thought it was hilarious and leapt at the glass. Rosie reared up and hissed. Barry – tiny – arched his back and didn't flinch. He was fascinated by this new, strange, caterwauling creature beyond the glass. He showed no signs of aggression, just a steadfast determination not to show submission. Rosie crouched down and continued to hiss and howl like a demented banshee. I felt slightly sorry for her, but in the shifting world of domestic cat politics, you live and die by the sword. In our house and garden, Rosie had had her time; now she had to let go and concede the territory to the new resident.

The two of them continued to face each other off for ages and Barry got braver. He ran backwards and forwards across the bi-folds and each time he passed Rosie he swatted the glass with a paw. She stayed crouched down, looking at him, hate in her big round eyes, hissing at each mock incursion. I was proud of Barry. His behaviour suggested that he would not be pushed around, which was encouraging.

***

Over the weeks, we discovered he had several quirks. He had a penchant for water, a fetish for anything made from foam rubber, an aversion to flowers and a destructive streak when it came to cups, glasses and vases.

Whenever there was a tap turned on somewhere in the house, Barry's keen ears would pick out the noise of running water and he would run to the source and claw furiously at it, and then drink from it, snorting water up his nose and sneezing it out. When we had showers and baths, we were often joined by Barry, who would sit on the edge of the tub. On several occasions he attempted to climb up the shower curtain and brought it crashing in on us.

Eventually, after he found his way up the stairs, the no-bedroom rule became impractical, so we caved in. Barry enjoyed rooting through any open drawers and discovered a stash of foam earplugs, which he chewed through with vigour. On several occasions we had to prise his jaws open and retrieve them. One afternoon he found a pair of discarded earplugs under the bed and swallowed them. Later, he stood in the middle of the kitchen contorting and making a low moaning noise while I was cooking. Then he projectile vomited two puddles of lumpy thin digestive gunk onto the floor. In the middle of each slick sat an intact yellow earplug.

Clearing up after him became a regular chore. The more he grew, the more of a handful he became. He'd fish teabags out of cups and lemon slices and ice cubes out of glasses. He hated anything fizzy and would attack any glass or beaker that had a carbonated drink in it. We lost most of our glassware and several bits of china.

Stephanie owned an antique glass vase that had been given to her by her grandmother, who had taken it with her when she fled the Nazis from her home in Poland just before the Second World War. That vase survived the SS, the Holocaust and the Toxteth riots, but it didn't survive Barry's flower fixation. He knocked it off the window ledge while he was chewing his way through a carnation. He liked toilets too, and would attempt to drink from them or fish unflushed loo paper from them.

The realisation that we had possibly invited a lunatic into our home dawned slowly. As Barry grew, so did his strengths and quirks. He wasn't like a normal cat. He displayed all kinds of conflicting behaviour. On the one hand he was as soppy as a puppy dog and craved affection. He loved curling up between us when we sat on the sofa in the evening, and at night his favourite place to sleep was nestled between my legs or in the crook of my arm. He just wanted to be around people, specifically me. The old refrain, "He loves his daddy," was often repeated. While I still maintained that cats were not capable of love as humans experienced it, Barry was definitely more affectionate than any other cat Stephanie or I had known. He really did want to be around us all the time. Whereas Alvin had been his own master and had become independent quickly, Barry craved closeness and contact. He followed us around the house and was inquisitive about everything. He stuck his nose in everywhere. If we were cooking, he wanted to see what was being prepared. If I was working, he would sit by my legs meowing until I picked him up and put him on the desk where he would wander around, tip things over and generally make a nuisance of himself.

And then, on the other hand, Barry was also capable of bouts of uninhibited violence. It was partly my fault – I never shied away from rough and tumble with him, and made a point of encouraging his hunting prowess and physicality, precisely because I wanted him to keep the mice at bay and to exert dominance in his own territory. I didn't want to risk another disappearance. But as his claws and jaws developed, I began to realise that I might have bitten off more than I could chew. Barry, I feared, was no ordinary household moggy.

CHAPTER TWELVE

WE NEED TO TALK ABOUT BARRY

Even as a cute, spotty little kitty-cat not fully grown, Barry started to display a regard for the fineries of play-fighting that caught me off guard and often made me wince. He was nuts, and he worried me. Some would say he was just being exuberantly playful, and they would be right, but when that playfulness was expressed through claws that Wolverine would be proud of, and jaws with a bite powerful enough to crack a nut (which he actually did one day), the liveliness started to feel a lot like pain. Behind the adorable round face and the baby-leopard pelt, there lurked intent. His claws were like razors. In the early weeks the injuries were superficial scratches that appeared as thin red lines just after he'd lightly brushed me with a claw. They were such delicate incisions, delivered with a deft swipe, that half the time I didn't realise he had caught me. Then I'd see a trace of blood and the look on Barry's face that said: "Gotcha!" He only had to brush me gently to break the skin.

A favourite game of his was the under-bed-leg-ambush. This worked best in the mornings after I showered or at night when I was getting into bed – both occasions when my legs were bare. He knew my routine and he waited patiently, out of sight, crouched in the dark, eyes alert, ears twitching. As I walked past or climbed under the covers he pounced like a hidden tiger, his claws unsheathed and flailing in front of him. Sometimes he caught me, sometimes I managed to pull my legs under the duvet fast enough to avoid him, other times he crashed clumsily into a towel rail or piece of furniture as he fell back to the floor. Often I laughed at him as he extricated himself from whatever contraption he was wrapped around, not realising he managed to make contact, and then I would feel the tell-tale itch as I looked down and saw the red thread of blood rise out of a clean surgical scratch. It was like getting a paper cut, and then applying itching powder to it. My legs became a height chart to measure his growth. As he got bigger, the scars and scratches rose higher up. I started changing in the bathroom with the door closed, fearful that one day he would manage to execute the perfect airborne vasectomy. The only saving grace was that although I still suffered itching skin and raised lumps whenever he attacked, the reactions were quick to subside and nowhere as bad as they had been when we first got Alvin.

The decision to allow him into the bedroom came back to haunt us as each night Barry attempted to climb under the covers. He didn't want to cuddle up. He wanted to attack (or play depending on your interpretation of his actions). The only way to avoid his probing claws was to wrap the quilt tightly around ourselves until he got bored and wandered off. That was how we slept, like two Mummies, tightly rolled in our bedding.

As Barry grew, it was obvious that he was much more powerful than Alvin had been. He was also more energetic. In bed one night, we were playing "where's the mouse" under the covers. I'd been warned by a breeder at LondonCats a few months previously that this was one of the things you should never start with a Bengal because games would never end, but I couldn't resist. Barry was trotting around on top of the 7.5 tog duvet, hunting out the source of the light scratching noises underneath. His multi-directional ears jerked instantly to locate the "mouse". Occasionally, I grabbed his leg though the material and tripped him up. Barry crouched and sprung onto my hand underneath the covers. Then he caught my finger and bit down on it with a force that shocked me. I didn't realise that a cat could be capable of such a grip. Through a layer of hypo-allergenic padding, Barry had my finger fixed in his jaws. His needle-sharp baby teeth were clamped down like a tiny gin trap. Each time I moved a finger, he tightened the grip. His bite quotient had range. Even more disturbing than the force of his bite was his mannerisms when he was biting. He really enjoyed the sensation of a human finger in his jaws. He snorted, his ears went back and his eyes started rolling in his head. He looked like a shark in a feeding frenzy: ecstatic, almost orgasmic. He playfully ratcheted up the pressure when I tried to release myself, as if to say, "This is nothing. There's more."

When I voiced my concern, Stephanie suggested that perhaps I shouldn't encourage him.

"It's not normal for a kitten," I explained as I tried to swat Barry away. "He looks too small to be that powerful."

With any kitten you expect some scratches and some bites – heaven knows Alvin caused enough damage – but the one dependable thing about cats as opposed to dogs is that I never had the impression they could really do damage. But Barry was less than four months old and he had a bite force that wouldn't be out of place in an alligator's mouth.

I took a trip to the pet shop and started looking at the dog toys. I picked up a rigid rubber pull and started to test its strength.

"Is it for an adult or a puppy?" the shop assistant asked.

"It's for a kitten," I explained.

"The cat toys are over there," she ushered. In the corner there was the usual selection of small mice-shaped soft toys and sticks with lures on elastic attached to them.

I shook my head. "Nah. That's not going to do the trick. He's not a normal cat," I said. "He needs something a bit more robust than a feather on the end of a stick."

I bought a small rope pull designed for dogs and I tried to encourage Barry to chew that, rather than my arms. He wasn't interested, of course, and the pull went on the pile with all the other paraphernalia Barry had been bought and ignored.

As his playfulness increased so did his technique. He loved grabbing my forearm between his front claws and then twisting onto his back, in attempt to bring my arm down with him. He clung on, clamping down on flesh, then attempting to tear off chunks by jerking his head from side to side, much how a big cat would rip meat from the carcass of a fallen zebra. In between chews, he raked my skin with his back legs, kicking out like an alarmed rabbit. His favourite toy was my arm – always the right one. He knew its anatomy and explored sinews, bones and musculature with his little teeth. He liked to pluck my elbows with his front teeth because the skin there could be pinched. He probed for tendons and bone under the skin and ground his teeth over them. He was like a little piranha. But he was also controlled. If he really started to hurt or get carried away I stopped him. He knew the limits. He rarely broke skin with his teeth, he just quite obviously enjoyed the sensation of chewing. He was teething, using my arm as a soother. He only did it to me, and I let him because I derived a strange, unsettling fascination from watching as he went to work. It was like being in a nature documentary.

"This must be what it feels like to be eaten alive," I said to Stephanie one night, as Barry munched away happily on my radius bone. She was not impressed and pointed out that the reason Barry only attacked me was because I let him. But there was method in my madness.

"He needs to be able to look after himself," I explained, as I grabbed his belly and brushed him around the wooden floor like a cleaning cloth. He kicked more and purred.

The training sessions became more intense as he grew. As I had done with Alvin, I encouraged him to chase me through the house to build up his speed and stamina, which he did with vigour. He would launch himself at me from behind furniture, a pint-sized lion attempting to bring down human prey. He was clumsy, but bounced off most things unharmed. When the weather got warmer, he turned his attention to flies in the house and threw himself at windows and across worktops at any that had the audacity to venture into his domain. I ducked for cover in the office whenever I heard one buzz past, because I knew that in the next millisecond an angry ball of fur would fly across my desktop after it. I became very adept at saving work quickly, having learnt the lesson with Alvin that if a cat walks across a keyboard, it will inevitably manage to hit the delete key. It must be something to do with the spacing of their paws.

Barry had energy, velocity and power, but very little co-ordination or common sense. More things broke. He developed a fascination with earphones. He chewed through several sets and when we got wise to his fetish and put them away in drawers he'd watch to see where they went and try to open the drawers when our backs were turned. He worked out that when Stephanie or I came back from a run or from the gym, we'd have earphones. He waited patiently to see where we'd put them or if either of us were forgetful enough to leave them out, rather than hide them away. He'd punish any absentmindedness.

"Barry! What have you done?" became the house refrain.

His fascination for water didn't stop at taps. One Sunday evening, I was standing in front of the toilet doing my business before bed, legs astride. I looked down and saw Barry sitting between them, fixated by the tinkling sound coming from the bowl.

"No, Barry," I implored. But it was too late. In a flash he leapt onto the seat and skidded into the bowl with a plop. I didn't even have time to stop what I was doing and Barry, directly under the stream, thrashed around and jumped back out, dripping wet. Before I could sort myself out or do anything, he pelted out of the bathroom to the safety of the bed, where Stephanie was settling down for the night.

"Don't let Barry in, I've just pissed on him!" I shouted. We managed to catch him and put him under the shower and then spent the following half an hour changing the sheets and cleaning the carpet. I wish that were the only time it happened, but several months later Barry caught me off-guard again in the downstairs toilet and repeated his bog-diving stunt.

As he continued to grow, the damage he inflicted with his teeth was nothing compared to what the claws started to do as they hardened. Those thin red threads got wider and deeper. A couple got so deep they penetrated the epidermis. I started to worry that he'd puncture a main artery and recalled the story of Graham Foster, a cat owner from Streatham who almost died after developing septicaemia from a nip on his finger from his Burmese. The itches I experienced every time Barry bit and scratched me were evidence of the bacteria in his claws and saliva. I panicked that one night when Stephanie was away, after a particularly vigorous training session, I'd die alone in bed, riddled with infection, while Barry looked on, licking his lips, waiting for a go at my putrefying carcass.

As the weeks went on he became increasingly restless. I frequently caught him staring wistfully out of the windows, fascinated by the world outside. His presence in the house had obviously worked on our mouse problem as, from the day he moved in, we never heard another scamper. This however, happened more by osmosis than by any activity from Barry. He never showed any indication of rodent hunting prowess and we never discovered any dead or injured mice in the house. They just moved away naturally when they realised he had moved in. Still, I tried the old spider trick on him and presented him with one when he was little, which he dispatched and ate. In fact he developed quite a taste for insects and would greedily gobble up any flies he was lucky enough to catch.

By April the weather was warming up. We couldn't open the new bi-fold patio doors, though, because he was too small to go outside and if he did, we feared he'd wander off and get into trouble. We could also only open windows a fraction because he attempted to climb through any gap wider than a few inches. We learned from bitter experience that windows were a hazard after he made a dash for the small bathroom window, which led to a 20ft drop. I just managed to grab his back legs in time before he squeezed through the gap. He could reach every surface in the house and regularly climbed up to the top of the kitchen units, where he crouched just below the ceiling at the highest vantage point, watching the world below him. The kitchen opened out into a dining area under a vaulted roof with skylights on each side. The fridge was under one of the skylights and Barry managed to climb and jump from his unit-top lookout onto the top of the fridge where he sat staring up at the opening several feet above, meowing to get out. To placate him, I ordered a "cat activity centre", which arrived in several boxes and took an hour to assemble. The huge contraption consisted of an interconnected network of scratch-posts, platforms and fur-lined hideouts. It stood over 6ft tall. I hung some of his toys from it and tried to entice him to play on it. It stood mainly unused. Barry preferred the boxes it came in.

In April, LondonCats was back in town and I limped along with a bandaged right arm to see if I could get some advice from the experts. As I stood chatting to one of the breeders, Steven walked past with Stone in his fur-lined case. I winced as we shook hands and gingerly pulled up my sleeve.

"Is this normal?" I asked.

He recoiled. Under my shirt my arms were an angry mess of scar tissue, scab and weeping cuts.

"That really isn't good," he shook his head. "You need to stop encouraging it."

"Do you think I should find a cat behaviourist?"

"I think you need help," he said.

On one of the merchandising stalls, I found what I hoped was the answer. It was evident that Barry was not going to be a house cat, and I was glad. I don't think I could have allowed him to spend his days inside. We had investigated cat-proofing the garden further but, at a cost of over £1,000, it was prohibitively expensive. The stall at the show, however, was selling cat harnesses and leads.

I picked out a black one with a gold, Air Force-style insignia on the back for Barry. All he needed was a pair of cat-sized Aviator sunglasses and he'd be a real Tomcat Cruise, I thought to myself.

Back at home it was a battle of wills to get Barry into his new contraption: he didn't understand that it represented a limited sort of freedom. Having managed to eventually clip the lead on we stood at the backdoor together, side by side, like two astronauts about to step out onto the surface of the moon. I let him go at his own pace and explore the pots, flowers and garden furniture and he began to grow in confidence, marking places with his scent, tracking flies and looking overhead at the birds flying above. He was transfixed by the wonder of it all. He dropped onto the grass and rolled on his back like a dog, wrapping himself in the lead. We did a circuit of the garden and then went back inside where I took the harness off and shut the door. He sat by it for the following 30 minutes, mewling to go back out.

Over the next few days his walks around the garden became more frequent and he went out several times a day. Spring took hold, the air filled with flies and bees and Barry was in his element. I started to feel sorry for him because the world he so obviously wanted to explore was constrained by the length of his lead, which was only a couple of feet. He was desperate to run off after insects and shadows, but could only take a few bounds before his bonds tugged him back. It was also time consuming to have to follow him around. I came up with a plan and bought a rotary washing line to which I attached a four-metre extendable dog lead. This in turn was hooked onto his harness, giving Barry a 360° patch of complete freedom. The system worked, and Barry was strong enough to pull the drier around with him, but I'd neglected to calculate that the drier was over a metre and a half in height, which meant that rather than a four-metre diameter of freedom, Barry was at best restricted to two and a half and not able to catch all the flies he wanted.

After a couple of days watching him sprint off after things, only to literally reach the end of his tether, I ordered a longer retractable lead which gave him the run of the garden. He ran around for hours to the sound of whirring, as the lead unfurled and wound itself back in.

But this system was cumbersome, particularly when he explored the flowerbeds and bushes at the side of the garden and wrapped himself around shrubs. Each time, his plaintive little cries echoed out across the lawn and one of us would have to stop what we were doing and trace the lead through the plants until we found Barry at the end of it, tangled up in shrubbery.

When he became big enough and strong enough, I linked both extendable leads together, which gave him enough reach to get up the willow tree at the end of the garden. His early attempts at climbing it were clumsy but he loved the tree and showed no fear of heights. Usually the lead would wrap over a branch or two, which meant that Barry could leap from his perch into a controlled plunge. He finally was Tomcat Cruise, mimicking the famous scene in the *Mission Impossible* movie where the actor plummets to the floor of a vault but is saved at the last minute by the pulley system he's attached to. Barry, in his little black jacket, even splayed out his legs to slow his descent.

Sometimes his adventures were more complicated, and he became entwined in the branches and unable to get down. In these circumstances the ladder would come out and I would fight my way through the foliage to rescue him. He was always pleased to see me.

When the time came to take Barry to his appointment with the vet to be neutered, he was used to the outside and had also developed into an athletic and fearless feline. Once again, I wrestled with my conscience and worried that, after the surgery, the cat that came back wouldn't be the same as the cat that went. However, I was also hopeful that a reduction in his testosterone levels would also take the edge off some of his more destructive habits.

CHAPTER THIRTEEN

NO ORDINARY CAT

Barry survived his appointment with destiny and came out the other side slightly less of a male than he was before, but thankfully with his character intact, if not his entire set of reproductive organs. We continued to keep him confined to the garden attached to the washing line, fearing that he'd disappear if released. He grew big enough to scale the fence into the neighbour's garden, which he managed frequently, particularly when they had their guinea pigs out in the run on the lawn. Barry heard the squeaks and squeals, his ear twitched and off he went over the fence to investigate. There wasn't enough length in the dog lead system for him to reach the ground on the other side, however, so he hung in the air, flailing embarrassingly, looking at the strange creatures a few feet away until someone reeled him back in over to his side of the boundary.

I started to realise that it was going to be impossible to contain him for much longer. Barry had a desire to wander and explore and it was unfair to keep him confined. He also had a natural urge to assert himself over his wider territory, particularly as he knew there were other cats in the neighbourhood. In the house Barry was happy enough because he was the only feline there, but the house couldn't hold him and the only way he could let the other cats in the area know he was there and find his place in the feline community was by getting out, meeting them and establishing himself. This is one of the inevitable tests new pet cats face when they arrive at a new home. If there are other cats in the neighbourhood, one or other of those moggies will have territorial claims and the new cat must stake its claim to its own patch of land. Barry's problem was Rosie, who still made sorties into the garden and stood just out of range, hissing and growling at Barry, who continued to stand his ground and greeted her with curiosity. He needed to show her he was the boss of his own garden and he couldn't do that hanging on the end of a lead. It was an important part of his development. Studies have shown that some domestic cats will play out territorial disputes for years, squabbling and fighting regularly to establish their rights over other cats in the area. One of the most important aspects of an outdoor cat's day-to-day life is the ability to mark his or her territory with scent. Cats' lives are subsumed by an endless round of scent marking. As soon as their scents start to wear off, other cats move in, so cats that are sent away to catteries for a few weeks while owners are on holiday can end up having to reassert themselves when they return.

We still had concerns about Barry being free to roam in the wider world outside the confines of the garden. As a pedigree, he was a target for thieves. Indeed Bengals, along with domestic shorthairs, Russian blues and Siamese, were among the most popular breeds grabbed by the cat-snatchers. In 2017 some estimates put the number of stolen cats at 360,000, and both Stephanie and I feared Barry would become a statistic. We needed a plan and started looking at options. Firstly, like the protective parents of a teenager, we agreed that Barry would only be allowed out during the day.

"He will be under a strict curfew," said Stephanie. "As soon as it starts to get dark, he comes inside."

"Agreed," I nodded.

"He'll be fed in the morning and then only again when he comes back in the evening. Hopefully that way he won't venture far. " Stephanie added. "If he's hungry he'll understand that when he comes home he gets fed. He needs to realise he will get rewarded for coming back."

"And we'll track his movements," I said.

Stephanie raised an eyebrow.

"I'm serious. We'll get a tracking device."

I had started to look at ways of monitoring his movements and the most obvious was with a tracking device. I knew smaller animals could be tracked because I'd written stories about a scheme that tagged and tracked hedgehogs in Bushy Park near Hampton Court. Conservationists glued small devices onto them that fell off harmlessly after a few weeks. The British Trust For Ornithology also used small devices to track migrating cuckoos. The 5g tags were fitted to five birds in May 2011 and allowed experts to follow their migration routes from the UK to Africa. If technology could allow man to track small birds all the way to Cameroon, I was sure there was something available which would allow me to follow Barry over the garden fence. I was right. I discovered an amazing array of devices to turn pet owners into stalkers. There were GPS enabled devices that attached to collars and beamed signals up to satellites. These could be linked to a mobile phone app, which showed the whereabouts of your pet on a map to within 500 feet. They seemed the most popular and sophisticated but were quite bulky for a small cat. However, I loved gadgets so in the end, I bought a high-tech GPS tracker which claimed to be suitable for small dogs and cats. Initially when we attached it to him, Barry was unimpressed, even though I tried to explain to him that it was the key to his freedom. He didn't understand me, squirmed, then pawed at it.

He was confined indoors for most of the day while he got used to his new tracker. In the afternoon we took him for a walk on the lead out of the back gate, so he could acclimatise to the area and so we could check that the technology worked properly. We had avoided showing him too much of what was beyond the confines of the garden previously as we didn't want to excite his curiosity. The less he knew, the better.

What I hadn't released was that the device did not transmit its location constantly, so it showed movements in a series of jumps from one location to the next. It also had to be pointed towards the sky so the satellite could pick it up, which, given its weight and the addition of gravity, was perhaps its biggest design fault. As a thief deterrent it was also useless because all a cat snatcher needed to do was remove it.

With all this in mind, when the time finally came for Barry to break free from the bonds that had held him for the past six weeks and explore on his own, I was uneasy. I'd placed my faith in science and science wasn't doing what it said on the box.

We let Barry fly solo for the first time on a lovely summer morning. His tracker was fixed to his collar, he was satel-lite-connected, and I had his location pinpointed on my phone. I opened the patio door and urged him to take a step outside for the first time without his harness. He walked out onto the lawn just as he'd done countless times before and started chasing flies. Without the harness, he was much more agile and zoomed around like a maniac, jumping up at them as they flew past, twisting in the air as they turned to avoid him. He was in his element. I watched nervously for a while and then realised that he was making no attempt to go any further than the boundary the leads had previously confined him to. I didn't know whether he had been conditioned to believe that he was physically unable to go beyond the garden, whether he was scared or whether he just didn't want to. Whatever the reason, he was perfectly happy to stay by me, near the house. He even climbed up the willow tree that overhung the neighbour's garden and needed rescuing when he couldn't get down. When I called him, he came straight in and I gave him a treat.

Barry remained garden-bound for several days and I got complacent. I hoped that would be the way it remained: him happy to be a house cat but with the benefit of the outdoors, if he so desired. And then suddenly one afternoon I looked outside and couldn't see him. Immediately I panicked and called his name. I heard his reassuringly familiar chittering from the other side of the fence and peered over. The guinea pigs were out and he was sitting by the side of their run, watching them through the chicken wire. His whiskers were twitching but he showed no sign of aggression. He was just interested. While I was glad he had extended his range I was also concerned that the neighbour might worry about the new leopard-like feline sitting on her lawn, eyeing up her pets. The guinea pigs were squealing away but didn't seem scared. Still, I didn't want to cause any problems.

"Barry," I hissed, "get back here."

He ignored me.

I went back inside and came out with a bag of his kibble, which I shook to entice him. He looked around, so I dropped a few pieces over the fence and he jogged over to eat them. I put some in my hand and leaned over to offer them to him.

When he stood on his hind legs to reach up at my hand I quickly grabbed him and pulled him back over.

"Leave the guinea pigs alone," I told him. "You're going to get yourself in trouble."

He started to explore on all sides of the property but thankfully never showed any signs of interest in the front of the house and the main road. In fact, it became increasingly obvious that Barry was a bit of a homeboy and had no desire to roam freely. I monitored his movements constantly through the tracker app and he never seemed to venture more than a few hundred feet from home. Most of the time the map located him directly in the back garden, even when he wasn't. Which made me realise what a waste of time it actually was. One evening when Stephanie was away I had pushed my luck and left Barry out late. It was a beautiful, warm summer's night and as dusk fell I felt it was unfair to shut him in. But when it did get dark and I started calling for him, he didn't come. I tried several times, shook his food, whistled and clapped. Normally, I'd hear the tell-tale noise of him scrambling over a fence a few doors down. But there was nothing except the hum of traffic and the sound of songbirds roosting. I tried the tracker app, which was useless and went in search of him on foot. I felt the cold finger of dread poking at my stomach and tried to calm myself.

"He'll be fine," I tried to rationalise. "He's more than capable. It's not unusual for a cat to stay out at night."

But the shadow of Alvin's vanishing hung over me as I paced up and down the lane calling his name loudly, in that overly-expressive way pet owners sometimes use to call their pets. It was at that point, at 10pm on a Wednesday night in August, that I started to regret calling him Barry.

Sometimes when you own pets, you have to put your own dignity aside and do the right thing. My persistence paid off and after 30 minutes of searching – during which time I had to explain in a fraught call with Stephanie that no, Barry wasn't back yet, but that it was fine and he would be back soon – he snuck up behind me in the dark and meowed for his dinner. I picked him up and ran back inside before he decided he wanted to stay out any later.

After that incident, in which the collar tag proved useless, we sent it back to the makers. I toyed with the idea of replacing the GPS system with a radio tracker but as the days went on, it became clear that despite the one hairy moment when he rebelled and stayed out late, Barry was happy to hang around near the house. He liked our company and preferred to be where we were. Not for the first or last time did it appear that Barry was more like a dog than a cat. He loved his games of fetch, particularly in the garden. He loved sleeping on the bed between my legs or between Stephanie and me. He was like a dead weight and impossible to move. He missed us when we went out and ran to greet us when we came home. When I worked in the office, he came in, clawed at my seat to get attention and when I leant down to stroke him, he rolled over on his back to let me tickle the soft spotty fur of his belly. It was bizarre. Barry just wanted to be with us. He continued to have skirmishes with Rosie, who didn't seem to be getting the message that Barry was the new cat in town. She came to the garden less and less and when she did, Barry would face her down, despite her insane yowling. I didn't understand why she kept coming back. She was like a bunny-boiling jealous ex-girlfriend who couldn't accept that the relationship was over. The comparison was apt because she'd also put on weight and let herself go.

When I told non-cat people about my dog-like cat they laughed, but no anecdote described Barry's behaviour better than this. In early September we went out for an early evening curry in the restaurant over the road. Barry was out, it was only just getting dark and we decided to let him stay outdoors until we returned as we were only planning a quick bite to eat. It started to rain. The food had just been served and we were starting to eat when one of the waiters came over to the table.

"I know this is a funny question, but do you own a cat?" he said.

"Yes…" we answered together.

"…I think he's outside," the man explained.

We looked out of the window, and there, sitting in the entrance lobby of the restaurant, was Barry. He was soaking wet, meowing and he looked totally indignant at having been left out of the romantic meal. The party of women on the table next to us looked out the window too and laughed.

I got up to go and shoo Barry away. As I opened the door he ran into the restaurant and made a dart for the table where Stephanie was still sitting. I chased after him, accidentally bumping into another of the waiters. By then the whole restaurant had stopped to see what was happening. Barry had a penchant for poppadum and Stephanie waved one for him. He stopped to sniff it and I grabbed hold of him. I got the impression he was enjoying the attention and I apologised as I removed him from the premises and took him home, where he was locked safely indoors.

Barry really was no ordinary cat.

CHAPTER FOURTEEN

A HALFWIT NAMED BARRY

Barry finished the job that Alvin started and turned me from a felinophobe into a flag-waving cat fan. There was something incredibly endearing about his personality, which was quirky to say the least. He would forgive me for saying this, but Barry was not the smartest cat in the world. Far from it – at times I wondered whether he was a little bit simple. He had strange habits. For example, he could not pass a plastic carrier bag without climbing inside it and poking his head out the top. Sometimes he got himself tangled in the handles and ran off through the house with the bag attached, flapping behind him like a superhero cape. Like all cats, he liked boxes, too. Any empty boxes lying around the house belonged to Barry and he enjoyed climbing inside, crouching down and leaping out at any passing human. Sometimes he liked to crawl inside and stay there quietly with the lid closed, watching the world through a tiny slit.

He formed a strange bond with the yellow foam man-shaped stress buster toys that Stephanie ordered by the hundreds as promotional gifts for her business events. Barry loved them and would hunt them out whenever a new batch arrived. He didn't destroy them or chew them: he just took them away, hid them and guarded them. He would root through bags and boxes to find them and could sniff them out at the bottom of a backpack full of other items. Eventually, after we came home one day to find scores of them scattered all over the house in random places, it became such an issue that we had to put the boxes in the loft where he couldn't get at them. His actions did earn him an honorary place on the Laughology website in the About Us section as Barry The Cat, custodian of the yellow men.

He enjoyed being in the kitchen when someone was cooking. He loved the activity and the sounds, sights and smells. He often jumped on the surfaces to get a closer look when backs were turned, and was removed quickly. Like most cats, he was a fussy eater and despite my attempts to vary his diet, he mainly stuck to one brand and variety of wet food and one brand and variety of dry food. He did however develop a taste for raw veal and fresh squid, especially the tentacles.

A cat that appears to be a picky eater, incidentally, is not being precious. It is altering its food intake to balance the nutrients it needs at specific times. A 2016 study published in the journal *Royal Society Open Science* discovered that flavour has less of an impact on what a cat prefers to eat than the nutritional profile of the food. In the study cats were fed a range of cat food with different taste and consistency profiles – some of which was porridge-like and sloppy. The study found that despite taste and consistency, cats adjusted the choice and amounts of food eaten to achieve a particular nutritional outcome. They all largely consumed the same amount of protein and fat despite the very different compositions, flavours and aroma combinations of what was offered. The study proved that cats are more concerned with nutrition than they are with taste and smell.

Studies have also shown that cats fed on modern pet food were four times less likely to hunt prey than those fed on household scraps, which was probably why Barry turned out to be a disappointing mouser. He hadn't been bought solely because of his looks. Part of my misguided motivation of buying a Bengal was to clear the house of mice, which he had done by accident rather than design. It became apparent that with the exception of promotional yellow toys and flies, Barry was a hopeless hunter. He had freedom to roam, a takeaway restaurant with an overgrown garden just a few doors down, which I suspected was a mouse nursery, and yet in his nine months he brought home nothing.

It wasn't that he showed no interest in hunting. He exhibited the right behaviour. He stalked his toy mice and he still regularly attacked my arm with all the enthusiasm of an apex predator. He watched birds on the fence through the window and chittered away with his tail flicking in anticipation. If one landed nearby when he was outside he did the same, but never attempted to hide himself and stalk. Don't get me wrong, I was happy for the local wildlife, particularly the blackbirds, which came back and nested again. But I did worry that perhaps Barry was missing some part of his instinctive drive. Maybe it was because he had never learnt. He did show an interest, but did not know how to turn that interest into action. Often Barry would watch the TV with us and get excited by the animal documentaries, so we started to show him footage of big cats hunting. He didn't quite make the link though.

One morning Barry woke me to be let out in the early hours, which he did with annoying regularity in the summer when it started to get light at around 4am. I trudged back to bed and went to sleep after he slunk out the back door. Later in the morning, I opened the patio doors and saw him sitting on the patio pawing at something under the garden furniture.

"What have you got there, Barry?" I asked, squatting down to look under the wooden table. He looked very pleased with himself. Something small and white caught my eyes. I reached under and flicked it out. Barry pounced on it. I shook my head in disbelief and disappointment. Barry had brought home his first mouse, but it was caught in a trap and was already dead. That's how lazy he was – he let someone else do the killing.

"Are you proud of yourself?" I tutted.

A few weeks later I discovered another mouse in the patio, but that one had been mutilated almost beyond recognition and I suspected Barry had again found it somewhere, rather than hunting it down.

Eventually he did strike a live target, but even then he chose an easy victim. Embarrassingly he picked it off from the neighbour's garden. They explained that they had caught him trying to climb over the garden fence with their partly tame pigeon in his mouth. They had a covered wooden bird table on their lawn and topped it up with seed every day. One particular wood pigeon had been returning for years. It was old, couldn't fly too far without needing a rest and walked with a limp. Barry had taken to waiting in the flowerbeds by the side of the lawn watching the birds. Spying the easy target, he struck and managed to get his mouth on the straggler. It fought back, got free but couldn't get away. It was too big for Barry to carry and the neighbours saved it from him and took it to The Wildlife Aid Foundation, so at least I knew it was in good hands. I apologised profusely and berated Barry for picking on the elderly and infirm.

Unfortunately, his attack on the neighbour's tame disabled pigeon gave him a taste for game and a little while later I caught him picking his way through a clump of feathers on the lawn. They looked as if they had come from a wing and had some blood and gore attached to them, which Barry was eagerly pulling off with his front teeth. They were grey and white so I suspected they had come from a pigeon. I cleared up the mess, much to Barry's chagrin. He was literally spitting feathers and sulked away over the back wall.

Fifteen minutes later I was inside the house working when I heard Stephanie call out from the garden.

"Oh God Barry, that's disgusting!"

I walked out to see what he'd done and found him standing on the patio with a large whole dead wood pigeon clamped in his jaws. And it was in a terrible mess, dripping with blood and viscera. I almost gagged. Its head was battered and immediately I realised that it had been killed by something other than Barry. Perhaps it had been the victim of an accident, possibly road kill or, more worryingly, it may have been baited with poison and placed somewhere by a cat or fox hater. By the look of it, the poor bird's demise had been recent.

"You'll have to take it off him," Stephanie directed, her hand over her mouth in disgust.

There was no way I was touching it so I ran inside, grabbed a carrier bag to put it in and a pair of Marigolds and crouched down next to Barry, who was standing dead still with it in his mouth. His head hunched down and he was looking at me with hooded eyes, as if to say: "Don't you dare."

"Good boy. Give it here," I soothed as I reached out towards it.

That's when I heard the sound. I had never heard it from Barry or any other cat before. He was growling at me. It was a very low, quiet growl, but a growl nonetheless. There wasn't any real intent from it. He was just making his intentions known. He wanted that dead pigeon for his tea. He had obviously found it somewhere, grabbed the piece of wing first, enjoyed that and gone off to get the rest. Remarkably he'd managed to scale the back fence with it in his mouth.

"Sorry Barry, but you can't have that, you don't know where it's been," I said as I tugged it free from his jaws. He gave it up reluctantly and I put it in the carrier bag, tied it tightly and put it in the bin. Barry looked on reproachfully.

He finally fulfilled his rodent-hunting destiny later in the summer when he arrived in the garden with a live mouse in his mouth. But, being Barry, even that wasn't straightforward. We were hosting a garden party for friends and neighbours, enjoying the late summer sunshine and a few glasses of wine. Barry had been in and out of the garden throughout the afternoon, saying hello to the guests, looking for attention and generally trying to involve himself in the festivities. I realised he'd brought a little present back when I heard one of the female guests shriek. And then another.

"Ew, he's got a mouse!" someone squealed.

Our friends from the village are quite posh – I'm not sure how much they appreciated Barry's interpretation of the bring-a-bottle policy. He walked into the middle of a throng of people and dropped the mouse, which immediately tried to escape. There were more shrieks. Barry pounced, then tossed the poor animal in the air with a flick of his head. It nearly landed in someone's Pimms. Barry ran off after it as it attempted to escape, bumping in to people as he went, focused on the mouse and nothing else. Along with Sarah's son Joseph, who worked on a nearby farm, I cornered Barry, who had the mouse back in his teeth. Once again, when I leaned down to get him, he started to growl.

"Come have a listen to this," I called to Stephanie, who was apologising for Barry's behaviour.

"Never mind that, just get him out of the garden," she exclaimed.

Joseph intervened, grabbed hold of the cat and mouse and took them outside where he managed to extricate the mouse.

Later, when the party was over, Barry came back minus any rodents and sat in the lounge with us. Usually he sat on the armchair he had claimed for his own or under the coffee table on the rug, which he liked to knead with his front paws. But that night he jumped up next to me and snuggled into my leg, lying half-on and half-off me. I stroked him gently and couldn't help smiling. It was a natural reaction whenever he showed affection.

***

I wondered at my conversion, but really it wasn't as surprising as it appeared. Barry and Alvin had done what cats have been doing for 10,000 years and continue to do today: subverting us humans to bend to their will by force of character. Cats were in the ascendancy. They were more popular than ever and although in 2018 they still lagged behind dogs in terms of national pet ownership figures (26 per cent of households owned dogs compared with 18 per cent for cats), I had a theory that the tide could well be turning thanks to two important factors. Firstly, as Ewa from the cat café and Steven from LondonCats had indicated, cats are more popular with Millennials. My theory followed that habitually, people tend to have a preference for the type of pet their family owned when they were children. Formerly, I had preferred dogs because we had dogs when I was young. If the younger generation now prefer cats, it stands to reason that a cat preference will be passed on to subsequent generations.

The main reason cats have managed to hijack 21st Century human culture, however, is down to their clever manipulation of the internet. They were, to my mind, the first non-Sapiens to use the web as a tool for species advancement, cunningly tricking us into posting adorable videos of them online, which we find irresistible and which then go viral. In 2014, Britons shared more than 3.8 million cat pictures and videos every day, and twice the number of selfies. The result of this fascination, say experts, has been a spike in feline adoption.

In 2015, the feline digital takeover received its own exhibition at the Museum of the Moving Image in New York.

"For some reason, cats took off, and then it's this avalanche that just sort of keeps piling up," curator Jason Eppink told the *New York Times*. "People on the web are more likely to post a cat than another animal, because it sort of perpetuates itself. It becomes a self-fulfilling prophecy."

According to historians, the first example of a cat video was shot by Thomas Edison in 1894 and showed two cats in a boxing ring wearing boxing gloves and sparring. The internet takeover, however, started 20 years ago in online chatrooms, and was launched by a particular community of people who posted photographs and used something called Meowspeak, a baby-talk dialect, to impersonate what they thought their cats were saying. The phenomenon evolved into a specific type of meme called LOLcats that were commonly designed to be shared on imageboards and internet forums and eventually, as the digital world developed, on websites. Legend has it that in early 2007, after a bad day at work, Hawaiian software developer Eric Nakagawa asked his friend Kari Unebasami to send him something to cheer him up. She sent a photograph of a now-famous grey fluffy cat meowing the words "I Can Has Cheezburger?" For some reason the LOLcat struck a chord and Eric and Kira set up a website on which users could submit their own LOLcats and memes. The site grew and grew, and became synonymous with the LOLcat meme. In July 2007, internet entrepreneur Ben Huh offered to buy I Can Has Cheezburger, and along with investors is reported to have paid around $2 million for it. By then traffic was in the tens of millions of page views per month. The cat meme became part of the internet and when social media began to make image and GIF sharing even easier, cats were able to capitalise further on their early digital domination.

Social media has also allowed for another online cat phenomenon: the internet cat celebrity, the two most popular being Lil Bub and Grumpy Cat, which has his own merchandising range. Both cats have distinctive looks. Lil Bub was the runt of the litter and is blessed with a minor deformity that means his tongue sticks out, while Grumpy Cat's downturned mouth makes him appear permanently grouchy. It's no wonder that cats have been described as the mascot of the internet and the internet has been described as a virtual cat park.

There are all kinds of theories as to why cats have mastered the internet and dogs haven't. There is probably some truth in the idea that cats do not strive to please humans like dogs do, which means when they are photographed or videoed doing something out of character, they are not doing it out of an eagerness to please, which makes the images more compelling. Prof John Bradshaw, a leading expert on cat behaviour, also believes that cats are a blank canvas on which humans can project feelings and emotions. He believes that since dogs are so easy to read, and cats aren't, it's easier to project yourself, others, or whoever you think is funny onto a cat.

I also wondered whether our love of cat content had anything to do with their unique stoicism. Cats seemingly don't care. They can take us or leave us. A vast generalisation, possibly (I only had to look at Barry and his affectionate side to know that this was not always the case), but in general, owners can let their cats roam without always having to consider them or their needs. A cat will please itself. If it doesn't care for its surroundings, it will bugger off, as I suspected Alvin had. If you have a dog and you are not engaged with it, it suffers. It is neglected. Even if you provide the minimum of a bowl of food a day, you neglect its other needs. With a cat, even if you don't feed it (which I am in no way advocating), as long as it's free to roam, it will go and find food somewhere else.

Cats can survive adequately without humans and we exploit that by shoehorning them into our modern, busy lives. We take them into our homes as kittens and adore them. Then, as they get older and start to exhibit their natural independence, we leave them to their own devices. The fireworks die out and we co-exist together. That doesn't happen when you have a dog. The dog is a more integrated part of a family unit than a cat is. A dog bonds with its owner on its daily walks. Cats get let out or come and go through cat flaps. A dog goes on holiday with its family, a cat goes to the cattery, gets fed by the neighbours or, thanks to modern technology, can now get fed by a machine. And that's why we like them. Deep down I wondered whether that left us feeling a little guilty about the pact that exists between humans and cats. Of course there are exceptions to the rule. As I saw at LondonCats, there were owners who placed their cats firmly at the centres of their worlds. There were owners who lived for their cats, which was fine by me, but I suspected they were the exceptions. For my part, I approached cat owning with a pragmatism borne from my fairly unique circumstances. I didn't enter into cat-owning with any enthusiasm, romanticised ideals or positive preconceptions. I entered into the cat-owning pact with reluctance and scepticism and grew to understand and appreciate both the positives and negatives of owning a cat. I had arrived at a place where I really did enjoy having a cat and understood how the relationship worked. However, I was under no illusions that the interaction between Barry and me, and Alvin before him, was anything more than what it was. I was objective, and by being objective I hoped that the relationship between cats and me was enriched.

Perhaps this possible underlying guilt was why the exaggerated representations of cats that we devour online are so popular. Maybe the memes and Instagram cats constitute the ideal, rather than the reality that exists. Maybe we want to be more engaged with our cats and to have more fun with them and laugh with them. And maybe deep down we realise that because of evolution, this will not happen. So we look at photos with silly captions and wish that our cats really were talking in baby language. Or maybe I was just overanalysing. Maybe a cat with a grumpy face is just funny because it is a cat with a grumpy face. Maybe, like the mug I have on my desk says, cats really don't give a fuck.

CHAPTER FIFTEEN

GETTING INSIDE BARRY'S HEAD

I had briefly met Jacky and Tim Bliss, who specialised in breeding exotics including Savannahs, Marguerites and Bengals, at the first LondonCat Show I attended before we got Barry, and there were very few people in the country who were better qualified than Jacky when it came to Bengals, which was why, when I wanted to find out more about the breed, I got in touch with her.

Curiosity led me to contact her. Over the previous years, since my first days trying to work out how I could accommodate a cat in my life, through to the trials and tribulations of owning and losing Alvin and the decision to become a Bengal owner, I had strived to learn more about cats and to understand how me and a moggie could best coexist. Even for a novice like me, it was evident that a hybrid cat (the result of a union between a wild cat and a domestic cat) was a different creature to a "normal" cat. Barry was so different from Alvin and I wanted to know what made him tick. In order to do that, I needed an expert, and Jacky was as good as it gets. She agreed to show me around her cattery in Grantham, Lincolnshire, to answer my questions on Bengals and hybrids. She picked me up from the station in her Jeep and when we pulled up in the driveway of her home it was immediately apparent that it was no ordinary cattery. The land around the property was a warren of pens and enclo-sures and looked more like a zoo than the cattery I had taken Barry to in the past (or cat hotel, as they called it). Jacky and Tim's boarding cattery, where they looked after other cats, was in a separate part of the grounds to the large area where they bred their pedigree bloodlines. Immediately around the house, the enclosures were dedicated to the Purebliss breed-ing programme and contained some of the most striking cats I had ever seen. The list of firsts and accolades was impres-sive. The first SBT Savannah litter to be born in the UK and registered with TICA was born at Purebliss Cattery (SBT stands for Stud Book Traditional, and means the cat is the offspring of a minimum of three generations of breeding within the breed, without any mixing with other breeds). The first Savannah to be titled outside the USA was bred by Purebliss. The first unneutered Savannah to become Champion in the UK was bred by Purebliss and the first Savannah cat and kitten from the UK to achieve best savan-nah cat and best savannah kitten in TICA was sired by a Purebliss cat. These were just a few of the achievements.

Jacky led me to the back of the house and a courtyard that was completely covered with wire mesh. There were smaller separate enclosures within the communal yard and a huge cat wheel for the residents to run on, as well as a swinging garden seat for them to recline on. We stopped at one end of the property to look at some Marguerites. They were alert and agile and endearingly cute with pudgy faces and large trian-gular ears jutting from the sides of their heads.

Unlike their ancestor, the sand cat, Marguerites made ideal house cats, explained Jacky. "They are not wise to the world, and are very soft-natured," she said. Owners who bought them were told that unlike a lot of domestic cats, they did not like to be on their own and enjoyed having company. Jacky explained that at the time she had bred four generations of Marguerites down from the first wild-cat-to-domestic-cat pairing that created her F1 kittens (F1 being the first generation of a hybrid breed). At each generation, the 50 per cent wild blood of the original offspring was diluted. Domestic cats used in the breeding programme were selected for their health and temperament. The selective breeding had been done to ensure that the offspring produced had no problems with upper respiratory issues, which sand cats are prone to.

To the sides and rear of the courtyard there were other pens in which various cats and kittens lived, from F1 Savannahs to stud Bengals. It was heaven for cat lovers. And there was a reason for the beefed up security. Purebliss cattery held a Dangerous Wild Animal Licence because it kept wild cats, which were used in its breeding programme – Trevor, the sand cat, two Asian Leopard cats and a serval.

Jacky invited me into her kitchen, which was populated with several Savannahs, and made me a cup of tea. I couldn't help but think back all those years to the discomfort of being in Kev the Witch's house, and how, just four years previously, I would have done anything not to have entered a room with so many cats in it, but I sat happily chatting while they climbed over me and wandered around.

Jacky explained that Bengals could be highly strung and were selfish with their humans.

"They have so much energy and can definitely be naughty but the trick is, don't try and stop it. Play with Barry, have fun with him. Bengals have this spirit inside them that is not easily tamed. It is part of what they are."

She also advised that Barry's aggressive streak was possibly because he hadn't been taught manners. She was probably right. She said that usually, when male Bengals are paired with females, the females teach them how to behave properly.

After our chat, Jacky and Tim took me to meet their wild cats. The two Asian leopard cats lived in enclosures just off the main courtyard and were impressive creatures. Although they are shy and hyper-alert by nature, Tim had formed a real bond with them and they allowed him into the enclosure without attacking him. They had mesmerizingly large, dark eyes and the flat, streamlined facial features of true predators. They were slightly bigger and longer than a normal domestic cat and much more muscular. I got to see the real difference when one jumped on the cat wheel in its enclosure with half a chicken carcass in its mouth and sprinted effortlessly.

Next, I was taken to the furthest corner of their land where the serval enclosure had been built. Jacky explained that it had been erected several years ago as a quarantine enclosure for the Norwegian serval that I heard about in LondonCats and which sadly had been destroyed before it could get to the UK.

I had never come face to face with a serval and was expecting an animal much like the leopard cats or sand cats, slightly bigger than a domestic cat and more exotic looking. I walked up to the large enclosure, which like all the others had a walled-off private interior and an outside run. There was a large sofa in one corner. Tim carefully unlocked the door to get in and shut it behind him.

I was totally unprepared for the creature that leapt over the sofa towards him in a single bound, letting out a yowl as it did so. It was the size of a large dog with sharp teeth and long legs. It had a small face and head, but huge ears, which in the wild (this one was captive-bred) would have helped it locate and catch rodents and small birds. It stood several feet back from Tim, who was in the enclosure with it, and sniffed the air. Tim threw it a dead chick, which it gobbled in a single bite. It was, without doubt, a wild animal, large, powerful, alert and wary. There was nothing about it to suggest any domestication. Given the size differential between the serval and a normal cat, I wondered at the mechanics of pairing them to create Savannahs. Jacky explained that breeding F1 savannahs was not without its challenges.

We left the serval after it had devoured several more chicks and returned to the house where, in the lounge, a litter of Bengal kittens and a litter of Marguerites were causing mayhem. One tiny little Bengal, just a few weeks old and the runt of the litter, walked shakily over to me and I bent down to stroke it.

"I'm actually allergic to cats," I told Jacky.

"So am I," she replied.

I laughed.

"How come you do this then?" I asked, gesturing to the kittens running amok around us.

"Because I've always had cats and they just get under your skin and into your heart," she said.

"How do you deal with the allergy?" I asked.

"I use anti-histamines. I take them all the time and have done for years. I've got no sense of smell left because of it," she said. It was quite a sacrifice to make for the love of cats, but possibly a godsend given the number of cats around the property.

After I left Jacky and Tim and the Purebliss Cattery, I thought about what she'd told me. Having seen the wildcats, I realised how much more complex and instinctive exotic hybrids were. They came with more needs. Unlike normal household moggies, which had the benefit of thousands of years of domestication, they were much closer to their wild ancestry. I made a conscious effort to engage with Barry more and to try and enrich his environment. If he had things his way, the waking hours between his considerable naps would be filled with play. But when I was busy, I didn't have the time. So when I got home I made some enrichment toys for him. I took a plastic bottle, cut some holes in it and put some treats inside. Barry loved pawing it around the room to get the treats out. It kept him busy for ages. I also found an idea for a cat activity box and glued cardboard tubes upright in an old shoebox and placed treats in those for Barry to find.

As Christmas approached I was gifted an opportunity that I felt would enrich Barry's life even further and give us a once-in-a-lifetime bonding experience. LondonCats was coming to town again in January 2018 and there was a household cat category in which Barry, who had never been registered as a pedigree show cat, was qualified to enter. I wasn't stupid. I knew there would be no point putting him up against the crème-de-la-crème of his breed, but I thought that against normal moggies, he might be able to hold his own.

In addition to offering the chance of a bonding experience, I also saw the possibility of a commission, so I called Steven and asked if he thought it was a good idea.

"Sure," he said. "As long as his vaccinations are all up to date," which they were. "Household pets are a key market we are lacking in the UK. TICA gets up to 50 household pets in some of the big USA shows. Here, we are lucky to get 10 or 12. People don't realise they can bring their cats. Barry will be welcome."

I mentioned that he was a show virgin and that he wasn't used to crowds. Not for the first time did I sound like an over-protective parent.

"Hopefully Barry will be able to stick the day," Steven said. "He'll probably wonder what the hell is going on, but the worst-case scenario is that the judges won't be able to judge him. Bengals are known to be very vocal but not very aggressive. In fact, unless Barry eats someone, he has a good chance of a title because he is in a small category."

I laughed nervously and asked if there was a contingency plan for cats that bolted.

"There'll possibly be cats that get loose on the day. You'll hear someone shout 'cat loose' and the doors get shut," Steven reassured.

A few days later I got confirmation that Barry was in the show and the nerves started to hit. Even though Barry was in the household category, he was still in with a shout of a title. In LondonCats there would be eight judging rings and each judge would whittle down the field to the top 10 in each category. As there were only around 10 household cats entered, if Barry behaved himself he had a chance of winning a title on his first outing. In cat shows, judges award titles which range from Master to Supreme Grandmaster. There was a possibility that Barry could be awarded one of the lower ranks.

In the wider competition, he would be up against some of the world's highest-ranking show cats. He had a chance to shine and show the world what a champion he was. I found myself daydreaming about the possibilities: Barry and I conquering the cat-fancying world. To add extra pressure I also agreed to write about the experience in *The Daily Telegraph*.

There were eight million cats in the UK which mostly lived unremarkable lives, roaming gardens, sleeping on sofas and defecating in places they had no business to be in. But Barry was going to be elevated to the other end of the feline social spectrum. He would be mixing with a different class of kitty altogether: the show cats from pure bloodlines who were whisked around the world in designer carriers, fed on expensive food, pampered in salons and presented to adoring fans on fur-lined platforms. I was concerned that he wouldn't fit in and that he might walk away from the event with an inferiority complex.

Barry was not a show cat, he was more of a no-show cat. He was mainly lazy but prone to wild mood swings. While engaged and sociable in his own environment where he felt comfortable, he could be nervous and shy around new people. His general demeanour towards things that were of no immediate benefit to him was one of indifference, punctuated frequently by unpro-voked attacks on my arms and legs. I feared for his ability to adapt to novel environments and I felt that, given some of his past outbursts, his conduct was in danger of falling well short of the standards expected of a top show cat.

Steven explained that Barry would be judged on his clean-liness, his character and his appearance. I had reservations, even though the fundamentals of cat shows are quite simple, particularly in the household category. All Barry had to do was stay in one place and show some interest when the judges tried to engage him. I didn't tell him because I didn't want to dent his confidence, but I feared that even that small challenge would get the better of him.

"Barry," I told him firmly one evening, "you are going on a training programme for the event." I wasn't quite sure what that entailed, so once again I turned to Steven for some pointers.

"Cats that play, get up on the scratching post and react for the audience tend to do well, as opposed to cats that have a difficult time coming out of the cage," he explained. "The event is supposed to be fun for the cat and the owner, so why would you exhibit a cat that isn't enjoying it?

"Try giving him a treat when he comes out of the judging ring. There are some remedies on the market that people use to calm their cats but if you have to use something, then I tend to think the cat shouldn't be there anyway."

I decided to try and get Barry used to the idea of standing on a platform and acting playfully in front of an audience. I enlisted the kids to help and used Barry's preposterously large cat activity centre as a stage. Millie and Lucas were the audience. I played the role of judge and attempted to entice Barry onto his hind legs with a jingly lure and some fishy treats. Barry sat on his haunches and looked at me suspiciously.

"Come on Barry, show some enthusiasm," I urged. The kids laughed. Barry yawned. Barry had always been quite particular about his toys and had never warmed to cat lures. I had tried several different types and none seemed to pique his interest. The only thing Barry really enjoyed playing with was an old bit of black cord from the waistband of a pair of my shorts. He would chase that for ages, so much so that Stephanie had tied it to her dressing gown so it trailed along behind her for Barry to chase, which he did. I got it and tied a treat on the end of it. It did the trick for a while and Barry jumped up, pawed it, chased it and ate the morsel. Unfortunately he only had a short attention span and so after three passable efforts, he jumped off the platform and wandered off.

I continued the training over the following days and also ordered a large carrier that was big enough and comfortable enough to serve as a pen that Barry could stay in for the day. It had a pop-up frame and mesh and nylon sides with a fur mat inside. When it arrived I erected it and left it open for Barry to explore. He walked in and sniffed around and seemed to like it. It had never been a problem getting Barry to go in a carrier so at least I could be confident we would get to the event.

I left the carrier in the kitchen so Barry could walk in and out of it at his leisure. I wanted him to be acclimatised and relaxed when the day of the show arrived.

I continued to hold regular training sessions, but Barry still struggled with the concept of posing and I began to wonder whether his lack of interest was indicative of a deeper lack of intelligence. Thankfully, a trip to the local bookshop offered a solution. On the shelves I discovered the bestselling book *Test Your Cat* by E. M. Bard. The surprise Christmas hit was a 1982 reissue and allowed owners to test their pets using a variety of behaviour observations and tasks. I bought the book immediately.

The book allowed owners to test their cats' co-ordination skills, communication skills, reasoning ability and social behaviour. Each section asked a series of observational questions about the behaviour of the cat being tested, for example: did the cat eat or request food on a regular schedule? Answers were on a sliding scale: never, seldom, often, usually and always. Each answer got a score. For example, in Barry's case the question "does he enjoy being touched around the face, neck or head?" was answered with "always", which scored five points. There were bonus points for challenging behaviours. Question included "has he learned to use the people's toilet, instead of a litter tray?" and "has he learned to walk on his hind legs for at least five steps?" Barry didn't score so well in this section. Finally there was a section of penalty points to be deducted. These were given for behaviours such as falling into toilets when the seat is up and falling asleep in a drawer and getting trapped.

I sat down with Barry and went through the book, observing certain behaviours. Was he able to remain totally still while awake for more than two minutes? Usually. Did his ears move while sleeping in response to noises around him? Always. After an intense half hour of observation his test results provided me with a glimmer of hope and revealed a respectable 116-point tally, which put him "above normal range". The score, according to the author who was a trained psychologist working with pets and people, meant that Barry was "physically well developed, co-operative, friendly and able to cope with most frustrations". There was even a certificate at the back of the book that I could fill out for him.

Buoyed by the revelation that Barry might even be a genius (or more likely some sort of cat savant) I decided to try and find someone who could help me harness his quirks and advise me on the best way to help him deal with the pressures of the show. I needed a cat behaviourist and after some research I found Anita Kelsey: vet verified, accredited and the only feline specific behaviourist in London. She had studied cat behaviour for three years at degree level and was a woman of many talents: she was also an expert cat groomer, the author of *Claws: Confessions of a Professional Cat Groomer* and a singer who had appeared as backing vocalist for Kings of Leon, Boy George and the Spice Girls.

"It's normal to expect your cat to feel anxious at its his first cat showing," she explained to me in a phone call. There were a long list of hazards that we would face.

"The car journey may stress him out a bit and he'll have to acclimatise to unfamiliar territory," she said. "The noise, the unfamiliar sights, being away from his safe, familiar territory, the sight and smell of other cats and too many people around him wanting to approach him. These could all stress him."

The odds, it appeared, were stacked against us.

Then Anita offered hope.

"But if he's used to lots of people, he may bounce back and want to come out of his cage and have a look around," she said.

That perked me up – Barry was indeed sociable and up until that point was unfazed by other people and cats.

Anita recommended that at the show I put one of my jumpers or t-shirts in the pen with him so the environment smelled familiar. She also advised me to create a corner in the pen where he could go for privacy.

"If you change the environment, he should get less stressed," she said.

There was one final concern I had which I was embarrassed to raise on Barry's behalf as it was of a personal nature. Barry had been neutered – or "altered" in cat fancying parlance. He probably didn't remember what it was like to be sexually intact and lived in a community of similarly sterilised felines. Many of the show cats however, would be intact. They are allowed to keep their bits and pieces functional for breeding purposes. As silly as it sounded, I worried about Barry's self-esteem. If he felt like a castrato in the chorus line of a virile Welsh male voice choir, I wasn't sure he would hit the right notes.

Anita had a solution.

"One way to eliminate the stress of being around other cats would be to line his cage with curtains, so he doesn't have to see the cats next to him," she advised.

Armed with that tip, I finally felt that we were fully prepared for our show cat debut. And even if he failed miserably, at least his pride would remain intact.

As the days ticked down to the show, I became nervous for us both. I'm not sure if Barry sensed it or not. I never voiced my fears and tried to spend as much time as possible with him so we could bond as a team. I wanted us to be synchronised, two parts of the same act, like Torvill and Dean or Ashley and Pudsey (may he rest in peace).

I phoned in to Steven a few days before for the last minute details. He told me that I needed to get to the leisure centre early to sign in and get settled. There would be a wire cage set up for me if I needed it. Barry would be assigned a number and we would have to listen out for announcements relating to our category. Importantly, I needed to clip Barry's claws, as judges did not take kindly to being scratched. Steven also mentioned that he would have a word with a couple of the other competitors in the row in which we would be stationed and ask them to keep an eye on me and help me out if I was struggling.

On the Saturday night before the show I got out my collection of grooming products. I had shampoo, a brush, a comb, some dry shampoo and clippers.

"I'm going to give Barry a bath," I told Stephanie.

"Good luck," she laughed. She wasn't taking our big day as seriously as I was.

I picked up Barry and took him to the bathroom where I ran a shallow tepid bath and tried to entice him in of his own accord. He looked blankly at me and then at the water, as if to say: "I don't think so."

I picked him up and gently lowered him in. The water only came up to his ankles. He stood dead still. I could tell he wasn't happy. I got a plastic beaker, filled it with water and gently started pouring it over his back. He bolted out of the bath in a single, clumsy leap and ran off to hide under the bed.

I went off after him and tried to coax him out. He sat there licking himself and looked at me reproachfully. I reached out and got him, then carried him back to the bathroom. But he knew what was coming and squirmed out of my grip. I didn't want to upset him so I decided he'd have to forego his bath.

I gave him an hour to calm down and then got the clippers to do his claws. I sat him on my lap and took one of his paws in my hand. He pulled it away. I tried again, but attempted to do it in one quick motion. He struggled, clawed at me and freed himself. I waited for him to calm down for half an hour and then tried again. He was having none of it. I made the decision to leave the nails as they were.

Finally, I got the brush and gave him a quick once over with that. It was getting late and we had a big day ahead of us so it would have to do. I stood back and looked at him. He looked just like he looked every other day. I had no idea whether he was show-ready or not.

CHAPTER SIXTEEN

SHOWTIME

True to form, Barry woke me at around 3am wanting to be let out, which was perfect as by 7am he would be at the back door waiting for his breakfast. It was a cold, damp January morning and he took a bit of persuading to leave. He had a habit of waking me, seeing what the weather was like and then deciding if he wanted to go out. If he decided it was too miserable he would trot back to the bedroom and make a nuisance of himself. Consequently, if I had an inkling that he wasn't going out, I picked him up and threw him out anyway, which he was unhappy about, particularly when it was raining. Barry hated rain.

As he slunk out into the garden and tripped the security light, I realised it would have been pointless to bath him the night before anyway, as by the time he came back in he would be damp and muddy.

I went back to bed but only slept fitfully as I was anxious about the day ahead. I got up at 6am and started packing a bag for the day. I needed food, bowls, blankets, water, a packed lunch, his brush, a towel to drape over his pen, a t-shirt to place in it, treats for him, and some of the toys he usually ignored. I assembled everything together and waited for him to return. Like clockwork he was at the back door by seven, peering through the glass hopefully, waiting to be fed.

He had his breakfast and a couple of meaty treats and half an hour later it was time for us to leave. Obediently, Barry got in his carrier and I zipped up the front. He looked through the mesh hopefully, like it was a game. I grabbed the handle at the top and lifted it. The carrier bent out of shape at the bottom and I heard Barry skid around inside. I hadn't realised that the base was not rigid – it was a slightly thicker material, but not thick enough to bare the weight of a cat, even a small one like Barry.

I carried him clumsily to the car where I realised that the carrier was also too big to fit comfortably in, and had to bend it out of shape even more to get it across the back seat. If Mr Bean had done cat shows, this is what he would have looked like!

When Barry was finally in position I got in the driver's seat and we departed. He started to meow after a few yards, which he always did in cars so I was not unduly concerned. Luckily, the venue was only 10 minutes away and we arrived and parked. Lots of other competitors were also there and I noticed that most of them had cat car stickers and very professional looking set-ups, with proper carriers, trolleys to pull their cats and equipment around on and vanity cases full of grooming products.

I grappled Barry out of the back seat and grabbed my bag. As I walked across the car park to the foyer the bottom of the collapsed carrier kept scraping on the ground. Barry fidgeted inside.

Once inside we queued up to sign in and were assigned our number. A friendly organiser showed me to the row where we were to be stationed for the day. There were several people already there set up and relaxing on chairs. Their purpose-made pens were covered in show rosettes, they had grooming stations set up and their cats were relaxed and comfortable. I said hello to my neighbours, one of whom was Russian, and explained that it was my first show. Steven had warned a couple of the ladies nearby that I might need a little help and they came over to say hello and go through the process with me. I had a show programme that listed all the cats and their categories. It looked remarkably complicated.

One of the women, Jayne, explained how things would work while I laid out blankets and a bed in Barry's rather utilitarian metal enclosure, which was on a table at waist height. He didn't seem too happy about being there and looked around in alarm when I plonked him in his base for the day. I jammed the t-shirt I'd brought for him in the corner and put in bowls of food and water. Barry looked through the bars, saw his neighbour – a very well behaved household pet named Henry – and hissed like a mean-spirited gremlin.

"Barry," I scolded. "Have some manners."

I apologised to Henry's owner and quickly draped a towel over the side of the cage that was facing Henry, so Barry couldn't see him.

Jayne told me that each of the eight judges would judge the category Barry was in. The judges were set up in the centre of the hall. Each judge had their own judging area, or ring, in which there was a table, a platform and a scratch post. At the back and to the sides of the central judging area there were small cages. At the front of the ring were chairs for the spectators. When Barry's category was called, I was to take him to the relevant ring and put him in the small cage marked with his number. He would then be removed by the judge who would check him over, have a stroke and a play and put him back. After all the cats in the round had been inspected, the judge would choose his or her top three. Points would accumulate through the day and at the end of the show, the cat with the most points in its category was crowned the winner.

"Once the judging starts, you have to listen out for your number. It gets quite busy so you need to be on the ball. I'll keep an eye on you and help out," said Jayne.

It turned out that cat fancying was far from catty. Several of the women in the row I was in could see how nervous and confused I was and took me under their wings, which I was eternally grateful for. Barry, on the other hand, was not impressed by any of it. His eyes darted around and when he caught sight of other cats, he hissed, growled and whined. I tried to talk gently to him and stroked him reassuringly through the bars.

The hall filled up quickly with hundreds of exotic and beautiful felines. Once I was sure Barry was as settled as he could be I took a quick wander around. There was every conceivable breed of pedigree cat. There were Bengals, Savannahs, Russian Blues, American Shorthairs, Burmese, Siamese, Ragdolls and Maine Coons. The owners were a mix of young and old from all over the world. There were the archetypal mad cat ladies, usually wearing some sort of animal print, there were couples and families and a lot of young Europeans. I spoke to people from the Netherlands, Belgium and France. There were straight people and gay people. It really was a melting pot of different creeds and cultures, all brought together by cats.

The public started to arrive, too, and were also a complete mix of cat fanatics, curious pet owners and cat sceptics who had just come along to see what all the fuss was about.

I went back to make sure Barry was okay as the room filled. He was crouched in the corner of his cage looking grumpy. I tried a pep talk.

"Listen Barry, everyone knows who the first man on the moon was, right? How many remember the third? Or the fifth person to run the four-minute mile? Or the seventh person to reach the North Pole? No one! You're a winner, it's time to start winning. Second isn't an option. Strive to be first. Crush the opposition." It was the same speech I'd given my kids on school sports day.

As I was stroking him to try and lighten his mood, a very well-to-do lady approached us.

"Is this Barry?" she asked.

I nodded. "Sorry, he's not really into this at the moment," I explained, as Barry sat with his back to the outside world.

"Bless him. I just thought I'd pop along to offer him some moral support. I read about him in the paper. I'm sure he'll be fine," the lady said.

In all the excitement, I'd completely forgotten that the story I wrote about Barry's issues preparing for the show had been published in *The Daily Telegraph*. I was taken aback that someone had read it and taken the time and effort to come and see him.

"That's really kind of you," I said, a little choked. "It means a lot to us."

"Do you mind if I have a photograph?" she asked.

"Of course not," I said. She took a photo of his back through the bars of the cage.

I had a chat with the lady and in the background heard an announcement over the tannoy.

"Household pets, ring one." Barry's number was called.

I apologised to Barry's fan and Jayne came over to let me know it was time for Barry's first round of judging. Flustered, I unhooked the door of his pen and reached in to get him. He let me pick him up and I held him across my chest and walked out from the safety of our row, onto the busy main floor. The walk to ring one was only a minute or so, but it felt like an eternity because Barry hissed, cussed and spat at every cat we passed. I'd never experienced behaviour like it and apologised again and again.

"It's his first time," I kept apologising. By the time I got to the ring, I couldn't wait to get him in the small holding cage and lock him in. He crouched inside, hissing at the other cats around him, who, to their credit, totally ignored him. I shook my head in shame and sat on one of the plastic chairs dreading what was about to transpire.

The judge was Steven Corneille. He expertly judged several other competitors first, all of which were impeccably behaved. Then he walked over to Barry's cage and I physically flinched. The startled, wild-eyed creature he removed only bore a passing resemblance to the cat I knew as my pet. Barry's hackles were up and his eyes were bulging. He growled and yowled at the cats around him. He squirmed in Steven's arms and clawed at him. Steven put him on the table, stroked his coat and gave him a quick inspection. Barry was in no mood to perform on the scratch post and wasn't interested in playing with a lure. He was placed back in his cage before he could do any real harm. The only positive thing was that he hadn't bolted, which I was surprised at. The judging continued. At the end, Steven announced his top three and then put stickers on the bars of each cage which showed the ranking he assigned to the cat inside within that particular judging round. Barry's sticker said "7th Best". I thought it was respectable for a first-timer until Steven Meserve came over and gently pointed out that there were only seven cats in Barry's category.

As I removed Barry from the cage the judge said to me quietly: "Please clip his claws, otherwise he can't go in to another ring." I apologised once again.

After another bad-tempered walk through the hall I put Barry back in the cage and panicked. How was I going to clip his claws? He wouldn't let me near them when he was in a good mood, let alone now, when he was cranky. And I didn't even have any clippers. It looked like our adventure was going to be over before it had begun. Jayne asked me how I was getting on and I hung my head and told her.

"We'll clip them together. You hold him and I'll do them," she said. She went off to get some clippers and came back with a purposeful look on her face. I got Barry back out of his cage and held him. Quick as a flash, before Barry had a chance to process what was going on, Jayne took each paw, pressed each claw out of its sheath and expertly clipped off the end. She was a clipping genius and Barry let her do it. He hardly squirmed at all. With his talons blunted, we were back in the game.

Barely 15 minutes passed and we were called to another ring for judging. I trudged through the hall, holding the worst behaved cat in the show. In the ring he hissed and growled at the other cats again like a pantomime villain.

"He's certainly got an opinion on events," commented judge Toni Jones, as she awarded him another bottom place. It appeared that not everyone loves an underdog, particularly when the underdog was a bad-tempered cat at a prestigious pedigree cat show. It was safe to say that Barry was failing to set the cat-fancying world alight.

In between judging rounds, I attempted to raise Barry's spirits with treats and strokes. I gave him more pep talks and tried to reason with him. He didn't listen and just sat in his cage sulking, occasionally hissing at by-passers. Several other fans who had read about him came over to wish him luck and take his photo.

"Come on Barry," I urged, "don't do it for me. Do it for your public." But the next two rounds were equally disastrous, with another seventh and sixth. The only saving grace was the fact that the morning raced by in a blur of apologies, hissing, disappointments and regular encouragement from fans who had come to see him. The girls in the row with us rallied round and tried to raise morale too.

"He'll be fine. Not all cats take to it straight away. He's doing brilliantly for a first-timer," they reassured.

And then, just before lunch, a strange thing happened. I was flustered and panicking as I had been most of the morning when a young man with a well-trimmed beard and interesting piercings came over with a hamper.

He spoke in a German accent.

"A friend has sent me to see how you are getting on," he said cryptically. He put the hamper on the floor reached in and pulled out a small, red, pillow-shaped pouch that was wrapped in cellophane. In the midst of all the madness, he seemed very calm, almost mystical.

"I have something here that will help you," he said as he unwrapped the pouch. "Put it in the corner of the cage or under his blanket," he advised, before taking a photograph of Barry and saying goodbye. I blinked as he disappeared into the crowd.

At that point I probably should have been questioning whether what I had been handed was legal. I had no idea whether I was about to commit some Lance Armstrong-type doping offense. Would I be cast out of the cat-fancying fraternity in shame? But I needed to do something to get us through the rest of the day. I was trapped between concern for Barry's welfare and my own selfish pride. We couldn't keep crashing and burning. We had fans now. We had responsibilities. "Screw it," I thought as, making sure no one else saw, I quickly slid the metal door of his cage open and stuffed the parcel under his blanket in a corner where it couldn't be seen. At this juncture, if it got him a ranking better than a seventh, I didn't care.

Barry sensed there was something interesting in his pen immediately and snuck over to have a look. He began pawing around and sniffing the floor. He sat down. His ears stopped twitching. His eyes started to close. I could see his shoulders relax. He rolled on to his side and in minutes he was asleep. I could have wept. For the first time that day he looked content. I wouldn't say he was happy, but he was comfortable enough to sleep, and I hoped that a nap would raise his spirits for the afternoon session.

I still didn't mention the pillow or the German stranger to anyone and, when the cushion began to emit a stronger and stronger smell, I started to worry that someone might get suspicious. To make matters worse, the smell closely resembled that of vomit. It stuck in my nose and when more people came to see Barry and wish him luck I had to usher them away from his cage and make excuses.

"He's asleep, he's found it very tiring so best not disturb him."

The smell got so strong I feared that Barry had puked in his sleep and choked on his own sick, like a feline Jimi Hendrix, but I could hear his slow deep breaths, so was assured he was still with us. Eventually, after he'd slept for an hour, I removed the pouch and went off to find a bin in which to dispose of the evidence. I later learned that the cushion was infused with valerian, a natural relaxant, like the opposite of catnip, and that it is used as an ingredient in herbal sleeping pills for humans and was perfectly acceptable for use in cat shows.

When I returned it was time for judge number five, Aline Noel Garel, the one who had flown into the show from Quebec and had her picture taken with Barry and me. Barry was fast asleep so I reached in and gently shook him. For a moment he opened his eyes and didn't know where he was. He looked quite happy. Then the sight of a huge Maine Coon being carried past made him sit bolt upright and start a low groan. He came to his senses and realised that the morning's adventure had not just been a bad dream after all.

After the strange incident with the pillow, however, his fortunes did change. He still made a fuss but Aline scored him a 4th Best in the next category and told me that he was a fine example of his breed. Then in the next round he scored a personal best and got a third. He perked up and started being a bit more civil to the rest of the cats in the hall. He still refused to show any interest in the lures and scratch posts but he didn't try and kill anything or anyone.

Later in the afternoon Stephanie came along to offer support and to see how we were doing. I showed her around and introduced her to the ladies who had been keeping an eye us.

"Has Barry been okay?" she asked.

"We've had our moments, but I think he's settled in now," I said.

Barry wasn't awarded any more last places and finished the day with a respectable 4th in the last judging round. His accumulated scores still placed him last in the category but as I packed his things away and got ready to leave, I didn't care. I was proud of him no matter what, and we'd had an adventure together – not one I thought we were likely to repeat, but an experience nonetheless. Barry had done what was asked of him and that was good enough for me.

After the judging round with Aline, each owner was asked to stand up with their pet and say a few words about their cat to the audience.

"This is Barry. It's his first ever cat show. It will probably be his last. He looks a bit dazed because he's been asleep," I half-lied. "He can be naughty sometimes but he's got a lot of character. The funny thing is, I never used to like cats very much. But I'm very fond of this one."

EPILOGUE

When I got home the night after the show, I made sure Barry had squid tentacles for his tea. I felt bad for putting him through something he did not particularly enjoy, but if you don't try these things, you never know, and he'd survived unscathed. I retired Barry from the world of cat shows that night and apologised to him. He seemed fine – the tentacles went some way to placate him. By the time I went to bed he was his normal self.

Most mornings, Barry woke me at a ridiculous hour because he wanted to go out. Usually he lay by my side, found my arm and started nudging my hand. Half asleep, I raised my arm and started to stroke him. When he knew I was rousing he rolled onto his back, held my arm gently between his paws and slowly pushed it away from him, then gently pulled it towards him again, with claws partially unsheathed, applying just enough pressure to wake me. He was play fighting and would gently nibble and lick. Whenever he did it, I lay in the darkness smiling. It was a pain being woken in the early hours just as the dawn chorus struck up its first notes, but it was also the best alarm clock I could imagine.

The morning after the show, for one of the rare times in his life, Barry slept in until a reasonable hour. He was either tired by the previous day's excitement, or still suffering the after-effects of the mystery pillow. When I eventually did get up, I let him out and he trotted off to do whatever he usually did in the mornings: most likely patrol his territory, lay down his scent markings and crap in one of the plant pots.

I made a coffee and logged into my emails. As I read down I noticed one from Anita, the cat behaviourist. And the mystery of the strange German man and the stinking cushion unfolded.

"Excited to hear how Barry did yesterday? I asked my friends from Katzenworld to pop by with a Valerian toy for him," she wrote.

Unbeknown to me, Barry's behaviourist fairy Godmother had contacted a German blogger named Marc Andre from cat blog Katzenworld who was at the show, and suggested Barry might need a little help to relax. Marc dropped by with some products, which included the small cushion laced with valerian. Thankfully, I had not infringed any rules and Barry was not going to be subject to any censure. It was a mercy mission and it had done the trick.

Anita's actions tell you everything you need to know about the cat lovers I had encountered on my journey. They are warm, generous, caring people, brought together by a common love of a very remarkable creature.

When I reluctantly ventured into the cat world, four years previously, I did so with my eyes shut (mainly because of the allergies). I had no idea about cats, their history, their needs and their personalities and frankly, I wasn't interested. But cats get under your skin and I started to realise that owning one comes with a unique set of responsibilities. True, they are not as demanding as dogs, but they come with their own special requirements and behaviours and, historically and culturally, they are still learning to live with us and us with them. As a domestic animal, they are relative newcomers and are 5,000 years of familiarity and hundreds of generations away from where dogs are today. Cats prize territory and often solitude. Their hunting instincts have not had a chance to be dimmed by time and they need to express these most base of behaviours.

Domestication, it appeared to me, has always been about bending an animal to human wills. Horses are broken in, dogs are trained, traits are selectively bred out from breeds' bloodlines. Cats, in the main, have stubbornly resisted our attempts to pacify them and turn them into something they are not, which perhaps is why we create our own versions of them on the internet and give them personalities and languages that we wish they have or that we project onto them. Meanwhile, in the real world, cats live with us, but separate from us. Of course there are always exceptions to this rule. The pedigree cats of the cat-fancying world are very much connected and reliant on their owners. But the vast majority of everyday moggies in homes all over the world are living their own lives, doing their own thing and are largely behaving the same way their ancestors would have done thousands of years ago. We like to think that our cats love us because we love them, but in truth, it is and always has been a very one-sided relationship. A cat's wild instincts ensure it always has the ultimate get-out clause (claws): self-reliance.

Stephanie and I don't own Barry and we never owned Alvin. We looked after them and provided for their needs. We made life easy for them. We fed them and gave them shelter but they were always free to come and go as they pleased and, as likely happened to Alvin, if something changed in them or their environment, or they could improve their lives somewhere else, they would go, without so much as a second thought or a goodbye.

I sat in the kitchen that morning after the show and counted up how many people I knew over the years who had "adopted" cats that were not their own. People who woke up one morning and found someone else's cat on their land or in their garden. In some cases, the cats stayed a few days, in others, the cats ended up living with them after they had checked for microchips and scoured missing pet websites. I knew at least 10 people to whom this had happened. And that was just me, so on a national scale it is not inconceivable to extrapolate that there are thousands and thousands of cats, fluidly moving between people who think they own their animals: a tide of cats changing their homes on a whim, breaking hearts and keeping missing pet bureaus in business.

I'd spent a lot of time in the previous months thinking about what it means to be a pet owner. I began from a point of ambivalence and had reached an understanding. We like to think that our pets are part of the family and that is partly true. They live in our homes and we shower them with attention and, in many cases, with love. But that love isn't unconditional, particularly with cats. We mould them to our own needs and in return, if they don't like what we provide, they leave us. Are they equal members of the family? Naively, perhaps, we like to think so, but The World War Two pet cull story proves otherwise, and while there are plenty of stories of humans putting their lives at risk to save their pets, most of us would agree that in a choice between a human life and a pet life, the human will win every time. Our pets may be citizens of our world, but they are second-class citizens.

In future, as selective breeding favours cats more attuned to domestic living, perhaps natural instincts will dim and felines will go the way of canines and become more reliant, obedient and eager to please. This is likely, and I'm not sure it's a good thing. My two kitties had not been easy and so many times I had bent to their will – they had never bent to mine. But in a world where man increasingly puts his mark on the natural world and subverts it for his own needs, their bold defiance and ability to remain what they were – not what I wanted them to be – has been both remarkable and admirable.

I finished my coffee and logged out of my emails. In the corner of the kitchen, the cat activity centre, or "tower of cat" as I called it, stood unused, like a monument to my own ignorance. Just because I wanted Barry to play on it didn't mean he would. There were no guarantees with cats. All you could do was try to understand them and hope they liked you.

I opened the door to the garden. It was a fresh, clear day. I could hear a few birds singing and church bells in the distance. I whistled and clapped my hands. In the distance I heard the sound of claws on fencing. A few seconds later, a lithe, athletic, leopard-spotted body darted through a gap between our garden fence and the yew tree by the back of house. In an instant Barry galloped over the patio, through the door and skidded to a halt by my feet where he looked up expectantly.

"He doesn't love his daddy," I thought, "but I think he likes me."

ACKNOWLEDGEMENTS

Thanks to all the cat people who have helped me understand what being a cat owner is all about. Particular thanks to Steven Meserves, all at LondonCats, Anita Kelsey and Jacky and Tim Bliss.

Thanks to Jo and Fergus at Mirror Books.

Thanks to Stephanie for introducing me to the possibilities of life, and of cats.

Thanks to my children, Millie and Lucas, for sharing the adventure.

Finally thanks to Alvin (wherever you are) and Barry, you naughty little boys.

ABOUT THE AUTHOR

NICK HARDING is an award-winning national newspaper writer and author. His work is published in the *Daily Telegraph*, the *Daily Mail*, the *Daily Mirror*, the *Sun*, the *Independent* and the *i*.

He has co-written several bestselling memoirs.

Reluctantly, he has become one of the UK's most prolific writers on cat matters, specialising in humour and quirky cat-inspired true stories.

He lives in Surrey with his wife and a cat.

Also by Mirror Books

The Boy Without Love
...and The Farm That Saved Him
Simon Dawson

Simon is a grown-up. He's officially middle-aged (if we all live to be 100) and has responsibilities, such as a 55-stone boar called The General and Buster the Billy-goat. But while caring so well for the animals on his farm, he begins to reflect on the distinct lack of care in his own troubled childhood.

Prompted by witnessing his ewe rejecting her lamb, Simon remembers his own childhood, with a mother who told him regularly that she didn't love him. Often that she didn't even like him... So what, he wonders, did he do wrong?

Both funny and heartbreaking, Simon tells of a latch-key childhood that involved physical and emotional damage, losing his virginity to a much older woman, failing spectacularly at school and burning his house down, while his mother entertained her explosively violent boyfriend and looked for someone she could give Simon away to.

The Boy Without Love is a comical, disturbing, compelling and uplifting read.

*Contains hazardous language. You have been warned...

Mirror Books

Also by Mirror Books

The Boy in 7 Billion
Callie Blackwell and Karen Hockney

If you had a chance to save your dying son… wouldn't you take it?

Deryn Blackwell is a walking, talking miracle. At the age of 10, he was diagnosed with Leukaemia. Then 18 months later he developed another rare form of cancer called Langerhan's cell syndrome. Only five other people in the world have it. He is the youngest of them all and the only person in the world known to be fighting it alongside another cancer, making him one in seven billion. Told there was no hope of survival, after four years of intensive treatment, exhausted by the fight and with just days to live, Deryn planned his own funeral.

But on the point of death – his condition suddenly and dramatically changed. His medical team had deemed this an impossibility, his recovery was nothing short of a miracle. Inexplicable. However, Deryn's desperate mother, Callie, was hiding a secret…

Callie has finally found the strength and courage to reveal the truth about Deryn's battle. The result is a book that everyone should read. It truly is a matter of life and death.

Also by Mirror Books

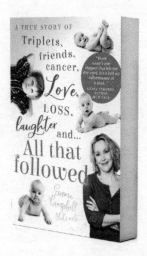

ALL THAT FOLLOWED
Emma Campbell

Emma bravely shares her uplifting true story of triplets(!), the embrace of friendship, losing love, finding love, the kindness of strangers, a constant fear of death mixed with the joy and relief of living. The anxiety of cancer returning… and then facing it head on when it does.

"There wasn't one chapter that left me dry-eyed, it's a love story…
a full on rollercoaster read" **Grace Timothy**

"Extraordinary" **Clover Stroud**

"Warm, funny… unflinchingly honest" **Amy McCullough**

"…a true fighter, survivor and inspiration…
she is someone I'll remember for a lifetime." **Peter Andre**